IN OLD PHOTO

LUDLOW IN 1960

DAVID TRUMPER

SUTTON PUBLISHING

Sutton Publishing Limited
Phoenix Mill · Thrupp · Stroud
Gloucestershire · GL5 2BU

First published 2004

Title page photograph: Bradley's clothiers and outfitters, seen from Castle Street.

British Library Cataloguing in Publication Data
A catalogue record for this book is available from the British Library.

ISBN 0-7509-3659-2

Typeset in 10.5/13.5 Photina.
Typesetting and origination by
Sutton Publishing Limited.
Printed and bound in England by
J.H. Haynes & Co. Ltd, Sparkford.

For my daughter and son-in-law
Victoria and Andrew Radford.
Happy memories of your first home together.

In his book *The Buildings of England*, Nikolaus Pevsner described Broad Street as 'one of the most memorabl streets in England'. This wide thoroughfare, which sweeps down from the town centre to the fortifications the Broad Gate, is lined on either side by a rich variety of architecture from fine timber-framed houses t buildings of the late nineteenth century.

CONTENTS

Abbeycolor Managing Director Adrian Madin climbs into his fully restored classic Fordson van, which the company used for promotional purposes. Abbeycolor was originally called the West Midland Photo Service Ltd, and was founded by Tony Bracier, Mr Madin's father-in-law. The firm is now run by a third generation, Mr Madin's sons Simon and Giles. Abbeycolor own thousands of wonderful photographs of Shropshire's market towns that were taken in about 1960. Prints from this book or from the company's vast collection can be ordered from any of its shops.

Opposite: The Valeting Service in King Street was advertised as the 'fastest service in the world, with branches everywhere'. It also offered 'fresh gay clothes without the expense of new ones, cleaned and well pressed at low costs. Plus Fabtex retexturing plus mothproofing free'. The frontage is the same but the shop is now occupied by Vaughn's sandwich shop.

INTRODUCTION

In his *Shropshire Gazetteer* John Raven wrote, 'There can be little doubt that Ludlow is the finest town in Shropshire. Not too big and not too small, busy but not frantic, it has good houses, good shops, a good castle and lovely countryside all around it.' This short statement describes Ludlow well and could have been written at any time in the town's history.

Ludlow has a history stretching back over 900 years. Before the town, an ancient road following the line of Corve Street and Old Street led to a natural crossing on the River Teme. A castle was erected shortly after the Norman Conquest as part of the defences along the Welsh border, and by the early part of the twelfth century a planned town had been laid out following a grid pattern to the east and south of the castle.

In the Middle Ages the town flourished and a great deal of wealth came from the wool trade and the manufacture of cloth. By 1377 the town was ranked the thirty-third wealthiest in the kingdom and its population had grown to 1,700 and it is from this period that St Laurence's Church dates. It was paid for by the wealthy burgesses out of their profits from the wool trade.

The town gained importance from the Council of the Marches, which was based at the castle and was responsible for keeping law and order along the Welsh border. The cloth trade still flourished and many of the town's timber-framed houses date back to this time. With the taming of the Welsh border the Council was dissolved and the town entered a quieter period of its history.

As travelling was difficult, the local landed gentry gathered in Ludlow for their entertainment. The town grew into a fashionable centre with many of the wealthy visitors erecting magnificent town houses in the Queen Anne, Georgian and Regency styles, where they could live during the social season.

Ludlow has always been the principal market town in south Shropshire. Today it acts as a magnet, bringing in tourists to view the many varieties of architecture in its 469 listed buildings. They can also eat at one of the town's world-renowned restaurants or soak up the atmosphere of the annual Ludlow Festival, held at the beginning of July, which has gained a high reputation in the arts world.

During the summer of 1960 Bernard and Bill Cross and some of their staff visited all the market towns of Shropshire to photograph hundreds of buildings and their shop fronts. This is their record of Ludlow in that year, showing the street scenes, the buildings, the businesses, the people and the vehicles of that time. Familiar names such as Bodenham's clothes shop, De Grey's Café and the Feathers Hotel are still with us while other businesses like the Ludlow Winter Garden, Keysell & Co. wine and spirit merchants and Robert McMitchell's fashion centre have disappeared. It also shows a quieter pace of life in Shropshire's most beautiful market town.

1

Corve Street

Corve Street. This is the main route into Ludlow from the north. It takes its name from the River Corve and is the longest road in the town, stretching about ½ mile up a steep bank from the river to the Bull Ring. The white building just below the garage is the Nag's Head. In the past, fifteen of the buildings on this road have been used as public houses.

This is the bottom end of Corve Street, which continues straight down to the left past the buildings, while the main road, Coronation Avenue, opened in 1931, takes traffic out of town towards Shrewsbury. The house with the two skylights is known as the Glover's House and is a timber-framed building dating from about 1592, with a later brick frontage. Dormer windows have now replaced the skylights. The building to the right was once the Trotting Horse Inn. It was first recorded in the eighteenth century and de-licensed in the 1930s. Note the hoardings for two famous drinks, on the left Ovaltine and on the right Guinness. The five is an upside-down 'G' indicating that 5 million pints of the stout was drunk daily.

The house next to the Trotting Horse is known as the Tudor Guest House. It dates from the end of the sixteenth century and was once the town house of the Greaves family from Culmington. The third storey was added during the seventeenth century. The tall brick building was used by S. Newing & Son, coachbuilders, but is now occupied by J. & G. Walters, who work in carpentry, roofing and renovations. The lean-to at the side has been demolished but in 1960 it was called the basket shop. The timber-framed house on the right was built in the late sixteenth century close to the site of the Lower Corve Gate.

Dot's Café and restaurant stood on the corner of Station Drive and was ideally situated for trade from the cattle market. The establishment also offered bed and breakfast and was recommended by the Cyclist's Touring Club, whose plaque is to the right of the front door. Kyte Learning now occupies the building.

Several people are standing outside Dot's Café. The hoarding used for advertising Super National Petrol on the side of the building is still there but the advert has changed. The single-storey building is the office of Morris, Barker & Poole. They were auctioneers, valuers and surveyors and land, house and estate agents and managers of the town's cattle market. They also had offices at Craven Arms, Knighton and Presteigne.

William Griffin ran his business from this small lean-to shop on Corve Street for many years. In 1937, just after he had acquired the business from George Gough, he was listed as a monumental and stone and marble mason. Emanuel Stead founded the works in about 1880.

Morris, Barker & Poole advertised in the *Shrewsbury Chronicle* that on Wednesday 14 September 1960 at 10.30 a.m. sharp an auction of 1,000 Hereford bullocks and heifers and 2,000 store lambs would be held, with a supplementary sale held on the Friday of 6,000 breeding ewes and store lambs. The pens on the left are part of the auction mart. One of the posters in the auctioneer's window is advertising the Royal Welsh Show being held in Welshpool in July 1960.

The auctioneer's office, the stone works and the house have all been demolished and the site is now occupied by Tesco's supermarket. The billboard on the side of the house is advertising *The Last Mile* and *Cash McCall*, two films showing at the Picture House in Castle Street. In 1960 the café on the left was called the Copper Kettle. The building was known as Belgrove and in about 1920 Thomas Flemons ran a greengrocer's shop there. By the mid-1930s Mr Flemons had converted the shop into the Belgrove Café.

No. 135 Corve Street is known as Streatley House and is now occupied by Sykes & Co., accountants. In 1960 it was the showroom for Chipps of Ludlow who sold a variety of second-hand furniture. In 1934 it was Woolley and Heath's commercial hotel; it also ran a confectionery shop in Tower Street.

In 1960 this building was the office for the South Shropshire branch of the National Farmers' Union. During the middle part of the twentieth century it was a grocer's shop run by Charles Corbishley, but today it has been divided into two small shops occupied by the famous Little Red Car and Mark the Nutty Barber.

The Nag's Head, built in the 1840s, was the nearest inn to the railway station when it opened in 1852. The inn contained a bar, smoke-room and tap-room on the ground floor and several bedrooms for travellers. The inn closed in the 1980s and until recently was a toyshop called Fancy That. The wrought-iron bracket that held the inn sign remains.

Peachey Brothers started their business as fishmongers at 7 Tower Street in the early part of the twentieth century but by the 1930s had expanded their trade and moved into these larger premises in Corve Street. By the 1960s they also had a shop in the Bull Ring and sold a wide range of fresh food, which included fish, free-range farm-fed poultry, and salmon and game in season.

The Star and Garter was first licensed in about 1822, and was also known as the Star Vaults or the Star Hotel. For a number of years it was the terminus for carriers' carts to Leintwardine, Broadstone and Vernolds Common. The inn was close to the new cattle market and in 1937 the landlord George Hogan advertised his 'excellent luncheons provided on market days' in *Kelly's Directory*. The inn closed in 1964 and in 1973 the building was converted into flats; three houses were built in the yard at the rear.

Bon Marché occupied the left-hand side of this building from about 1935 while Oliver Howard, a gun and rifle maker, occupied the right-hand side. At first Bon Marché supplied government surplus clothing but after extending its shop into the gunsmiths it began selling branded goods such as Tuf boots, Excelsior corsetry and Cherub clothes for children, as well as specialising in curtain fabrics and other household soft furnishings. When the business closed the building was again divided. The left-hand section is now Kaboodle Country Inscriptions while on the right is Bon Marché amusement arcade.

BON MARCHE

LUDLOW

Telephone: 616 — *Opposite* G.P.O.

"FINN" SHOES
"TUF" BOOTS
"EXCELSIOR" CORSETRY
"SOLARKLAD" UNDERWEAR
"CHERUB" FOR CHILDREN
"DAVID WHITEHEAD" FURNISHINGS
"FAITHFUL" BRAND JEANS
INDUSTRIAL OVERALLS AND APRONS

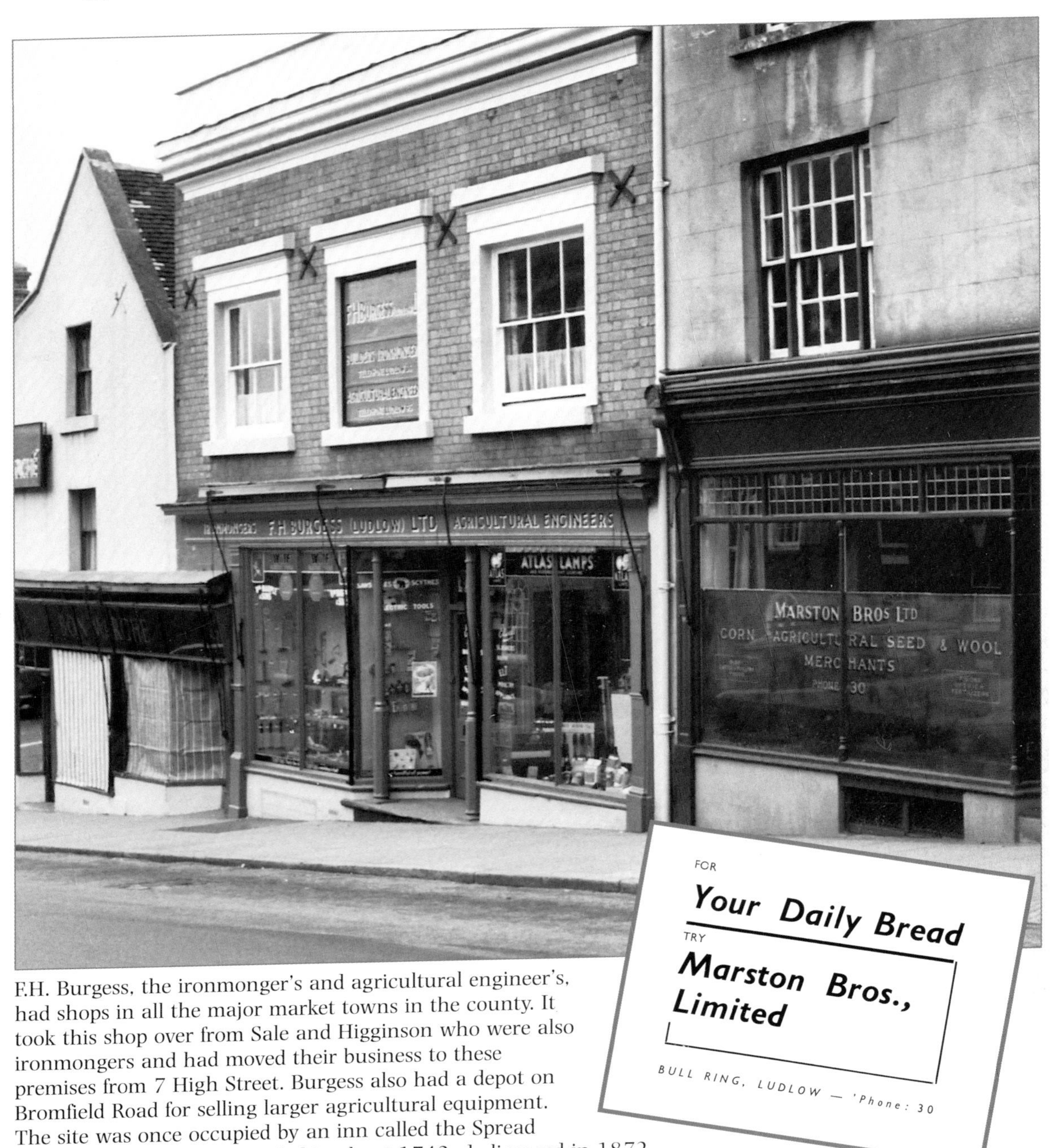

F.H. Burgess, the ironmonger's and agricultural engineer's, had shops in all the major market towns in the county. It took this shop over from Sale and Higginson who were also ironmongers and had moved their business to these premises from 7 High Street. Burgess also had a depot on Bromfield Road for selling larger agricultural equipment. The site was once occupied by an inn called the Spread Eagle, which was first recorded in about 1742, de-licensed in 1872 and later demolished. The Silver Pear gift shop once occupied this building. William Marston was a baker and corn and flour factor at 25 Bull Ring in 1871. His sons continued with the bakery in the Bull Ring, but transferred their corn and seed merchant business to these premises next to the ironmongers. At one time they were district agents for the 'celebrated Bibby feeding cakes and meal'. They also sold artificial manure and were buyers of wool, grain and seed. The florists Floribunda now use the shop.

J.H. Oughton's house-furnishing shop was in the last building on this side of Corve Street. In 1960 he advertised that he was trading from the 'Old Food Office' in Corve Street. He sold old and new furniture and good quality second-hand items at low prices. The gateway to the left of the shop now leads into the Parkway shopping area. The alley to the right is Wood Yard.

In the 1930s 12 Corve Street was occupied by Walter Steer, a hairdresser. By 1960 it was known as Estelle, a ladies' and children's hairdressing salon, run by P.J. Brown. The salon offered 'Jamal Machineless Luxurious Waving, The Kindest To Your Hair'. They were also specialists using Eugene, Zotos, Lustron and other tinting and bleaching products. The salon was open from 9 a.m. until 6 p.m. six days a week.

The photographer is practically at the top of Corve Street looking north. Many of the large buildings on the left housed offices or small businesses. In the 1930s there were several boarding houses in the street, including Mrs Langley's Boarding House, Griffiths' Commercial and Temperance Hotel and Annie Beddoes' Boarding House at no. 10. The stable block just below the first building on the left has been converted into a house called the Old Stable House.

Opposite, above: An inn called the Green Dragon, which was here during the Civil War, once occupied this site. It was one of three taverns in Corve Street left after most of the buildings in the street had been razed to the ground by the Royalist troops occupying the town in the hope of hindering an attack by the Parliamentarians. In the 1930s part of the house was occupied by Mrs Annie Beddoes as a boarding house. In 1960 the building had been converted into offices by Phillips & Co., solicitors, who are still there today. The telephone kiosk on the left has been removed.

Opposite, below: Ludlow's new post office was opened at 1 p.m. on 12 March 1926 by Col. G. Windsor Clive, MP for the Ludlow Division. The office was designed in the Georgian style and built by Messrs Drew of Stroud, using red brick and Bath stone dressing. It was fully fitted with electricity, was centrally heated and cost in the region of £10,000. The accommodation consisted of an office for the Postmaster Col. Wayne, room for six counter staff, a telegraph room and telephone exchange. At the rear was a sorting office and at the front of the building a stamp vending machine was erected. The Mayor, Ald. J. Palmer, and the Corporation were in attendance and it was the Mayor who sent the first telegram to the Postmaster General in London, bought the first book of stamps and posted the first letter. After the formal opening the party retired to the Feathers for a celebration lunch.

TELEPHONE

POST
OFFICE

Goldings hardware store stood at 3 Corve Street and sold a wide range of goods from birdcages to babywear. The building is now occupied by Clee Hill Electrics which also has another branch in Church Stretton. The building just to the left of the shop is the Compasses.

This house was the home and business premises of photographer Thomas Evans for almost half a century. As well as taking photographs he was able to make enlargements from old and faded prints using 'Platinotype and Carbon'.
He could also develop and print photographs from plates and film – and frame the finished articles. Mr Evans was also the secretary of the Loyal Countess of Plymouth Lodge, one of the Oddfellows' Clubs in the town. By 1960 the ground floor had been converted into a small greengrocer's shop and today it is an antique shop run by G. & D. Ginger.

2

The Bull Ring

This view looks up Corve Street towards the Bull Ring. Where the road narrows is the site of the Corve Gate, one of the seven entrances into town through the old town wall. The gate was built for defence and was flanked on either side by large drum towers; note the rounded corners of the buildings on either side of the road. In 1960 the house on the right was one of Ludlow's many antique shops, while the House of Quality on the left was a grocery shop run by Albert Gatehouse.

The photographer is looking north from the Bull Ring towards Corve Gate and Corve Street. On the right the Feathers Hotel has extended into the building next door, although the ground floor is still occupied by Maxwell's antique and fine furnishing shop. On the left is the Bull Hotel, an inn since the sixteenth century. The entrance leads through to a large courtyard where fringe entertainment is performed during the Ludlow Festival; a flight of steps also leads out of the courtyard and up to the church.

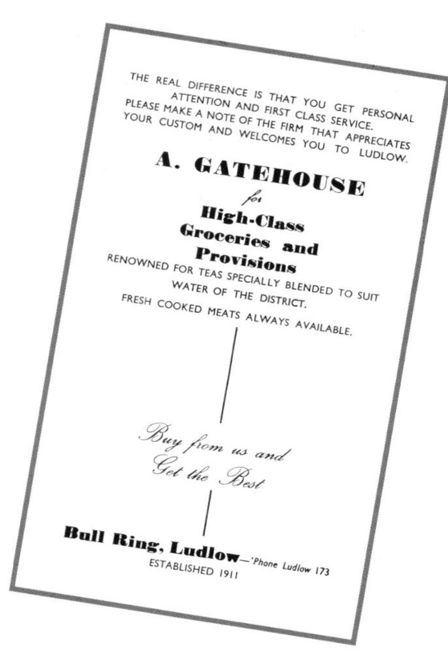

Opposite: In 1921 Albert Gatehouse had a grocery shop at 117 Lower Galdeford but by 1929 had moved to these premises. The firm was established in 1911 and we are told in the advertisement opposite that when we visit A. Gatehouse for high class groceries and provisions the 'real difference is that you get first class service'. They were renowned for their teas, especially blended to suit the water of the district. The shop is now occupied by Beaux Arts.

A. GATEHOUSE
TAILOR. H.
GATEHOUSE GROCER
TAILOR
H.F. HARV
TAILOR & OUTFIT

H.F. Harvey took this tailor's shop over from William Jones in about 1935. In 1905 Mr Jones had established his business in Market Street, Craven Arms, but by 1917 had moved to Ludlow. Not long after this photograph was taken Mr Harvey extended next door into Gatehouse's old shop. This shop is now occupied by the Feathers Gallery who make picture frames and sell oil paint, watercolours and a range of prints and maps.

In 1922 this shop was occupied by Miss Florence Palmer and was listed as a fancy repository. By 1937 Edith Small had opened a wool shop here but by 1960 it was occupied by H.F. Harvey who had moved some of his stock in; note the ties in the left-hand window. The name of the shop refers to John Milton's *Masque of Comus*, first performed at Ludlow Castle in 1634. The site of Harvey's shop in the previous picture and this shop was occupied by an inn called the Bull and Castle in the seventeenth and eighteenth centuries. The building is now used by Viners, a shop with inspiring ideas for interior decoration.

There was also an inn on the site next to Comus. It was called the Griffin and was open from the middle of the seventeenth century until 1721. The old building was demolished and this new one was erected in about 1840; it is now part of the Feathers Hotel. In 1960 the ground floor was Maxwell's antique shop but it has since been divided into two shops, at present occupied by Bearwood by Design and the Best Wishes card shop.

With its elaborately carved and beautifully preserved timber frame, the Feathers is one of the best known and most photographed buildings in the county. It was once the home of Rees Jones, a lawyer at the Council of the Marches, and his initials can still be seen on the lock plate of the main door. It has been an inn since 1670 and is now a very comfortable hotel. In about 1900 it was listed as a 'First Class Family & Commercial Hotel and Posting House'. It had billiard and smoking rooms, good accommodation for hunters and gentlemen's horses and an omnibus was available to meet guests arriving by train. The Feathers also hired out an assortment of horses and carriages, which included wedding and funeral carriages and hearse, flys, broughams and brakes as well as post and saddle horses, all 'let at short notice and on reasonable terms'.

This is Peachey's second outlet, which they opened some years after moving into Corve Street. At this shop they ran a delicatessen and were able to stock a full range of groceries and frozen foods. The firm also offered customers two hours free parking in the Corve Street car park. They had a restaurant, which they advertised as being 'tucked away in one of the many quaint passages in Ludlow', but it could also be approached through the front of the shop. There you could have a morning coffee, eat lunch or have a grilled snack between 12 noon and 2 p.m. and an ice or a cream tea in the afternoon. Boots the Chemist now occupies the shop. The bust under the eaves is supposed to represent Queen Elizabeth I.

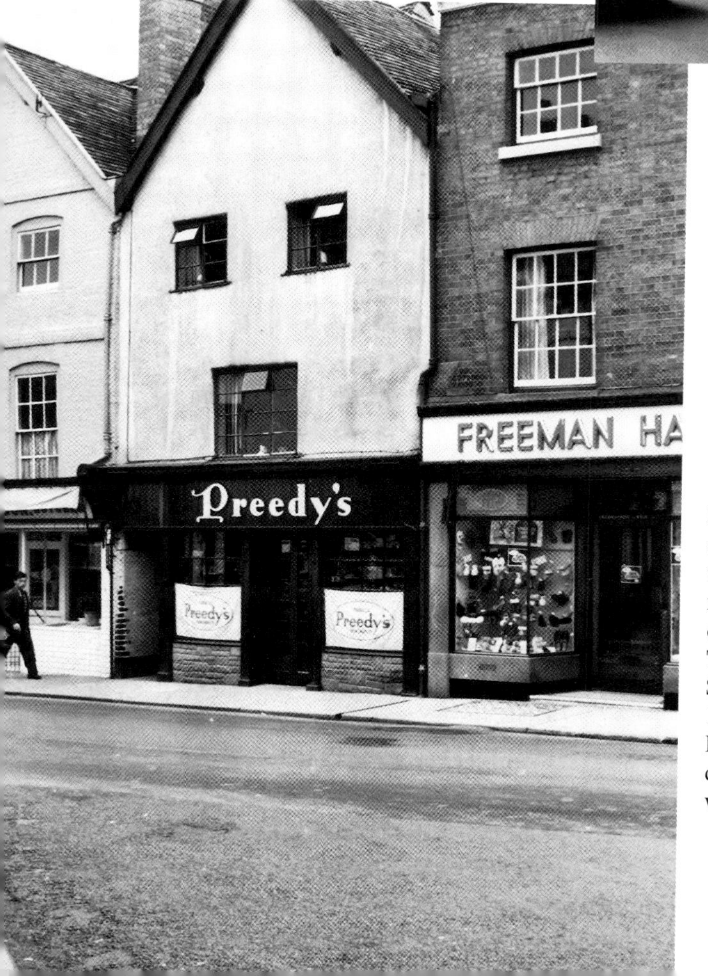

Both Preedy's and the shop to the left were once an inn called the King's Arms. They were later divided up, the left-hand side remaining as the King's Arms while the other side became a boot and shoe shop. The inn closed in the 1920s and William Sheldon moved his butcher's shop from 14 Tower Street to 36 Bull Ring. In 1960 Preedy's business was listed as a confectionery shop but is also sold a wide variety of cigars, cigarettes and tobacco.

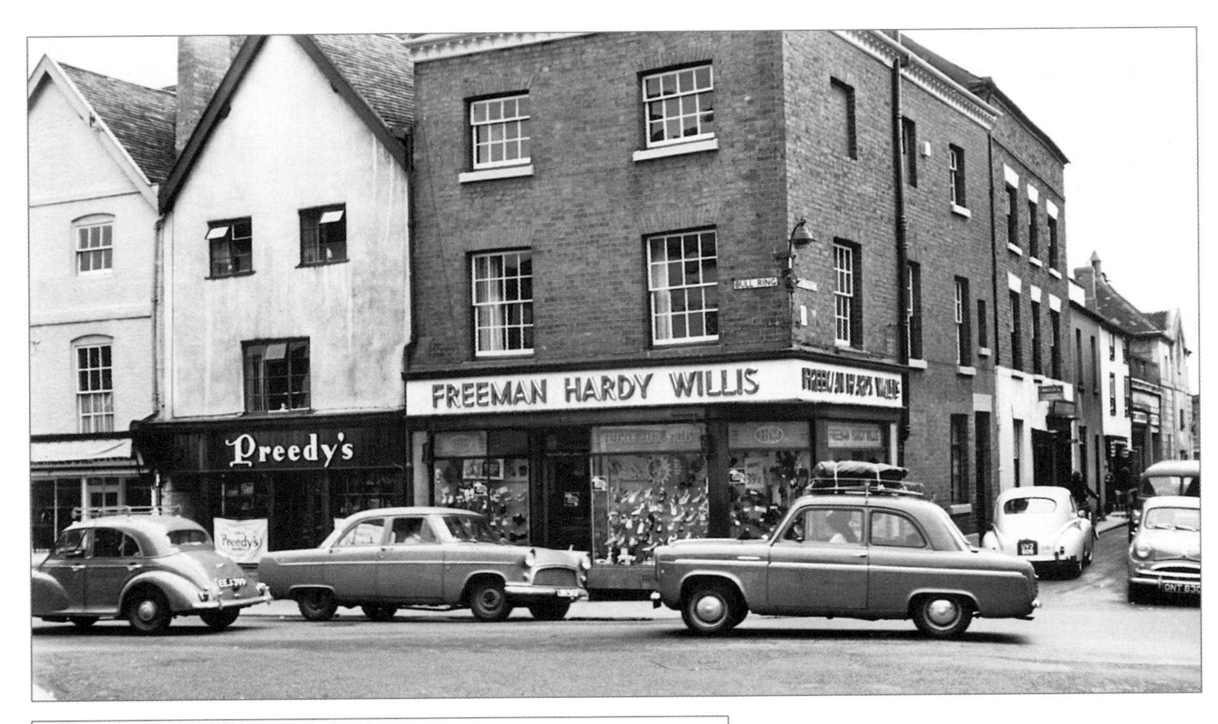

The firm of Freeman, Hardy and Willis was a national group of shops. It moved into Ludlow at the beginning of the twentieth century, opening a shoe shop at 6 Broad Street. It transferred its business to these premises on the corner of the Bull Ring and Tower Street in the middle of the 1920s, and remained there until the start of the 1990s when it opened a new shop in King Street before finally closing. The building is presently up for sale but the ground floor houses a shop called Style Collection.

The next three photographs show a group of buildings that stand on an island on the northern side of the Bull Ring. They were built at the beginning of the seventeenth century on the site of an open market called the Shelde, a corruption of the word Selda, the Latin for stalls. William Brown was first listed here as a chemist in about 1905 when he was also manager of the Shropshire Horse and Cattle Food Co. The no waiting sign has now been replaced by traffic lights for a pedestrian crossing.

For this view the photographer is standing with his back to Tower Street. Between the eaves of the building you can see the cross on the roof of St Laurence's Church. By the 1930s Mr Brown had started to develop and print films as well as supply photographic material to his customers. He was also the agent for Marston's Corn Eradicator and Brown's Extract of Celery. Note the posters advertising the Picture House, a carnival, a motorbike scramble and the Loton Hill Climb.

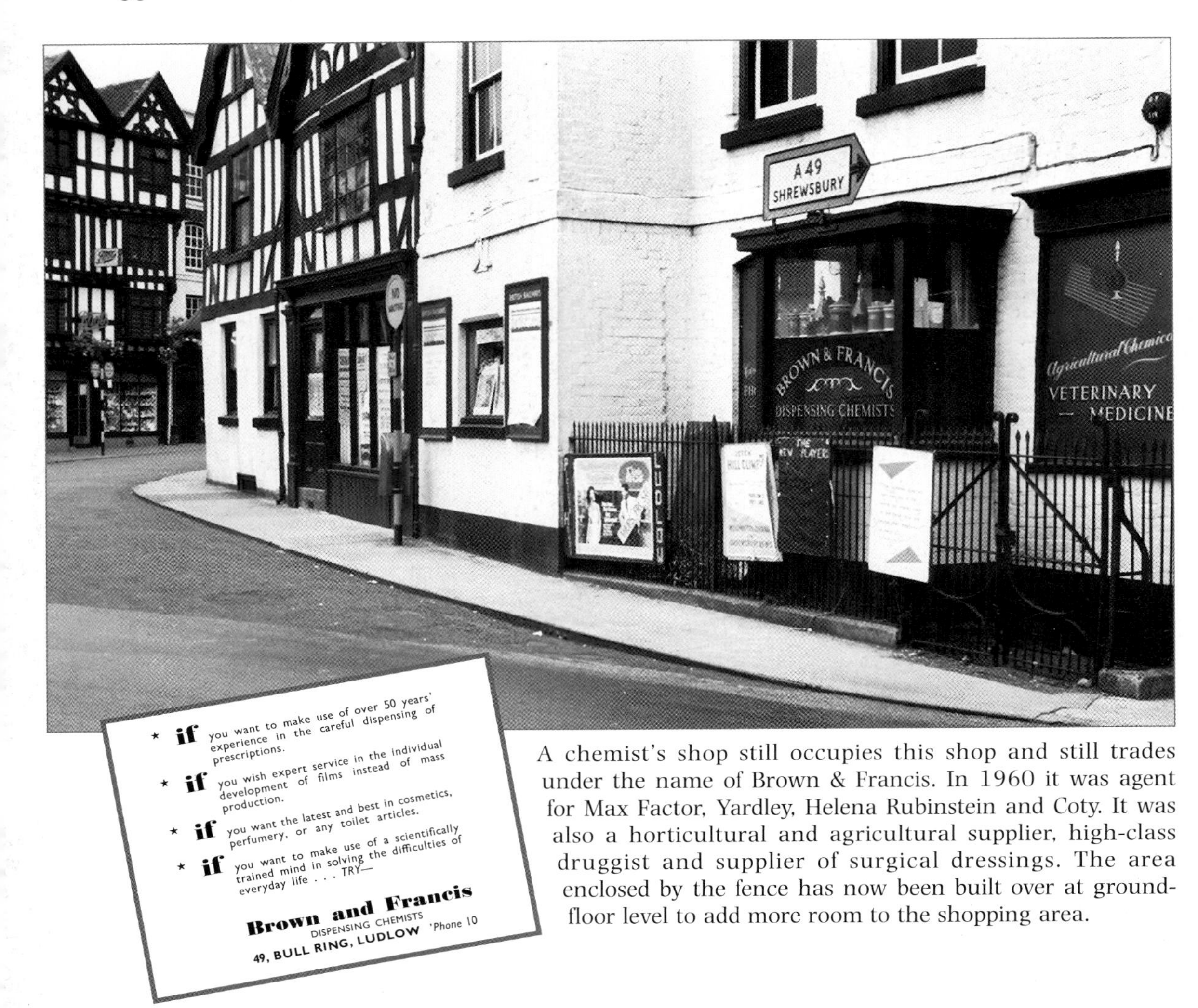

A chemist's shop still occupies this shop and still trades under the name of Brown & Francis. In 1960 it was agent for Max Factor, Yardley, Helena Rubinstein and Coty. It was also a horticultural and agricultural supplier, high-class druggist and supplier of surgical dressings. The area enclosed by the fence has now been built over at ground-floor level to add more room to the shopping area.

Opposite, above: The Bull Ring Tavern is housed in two fine timber-framed houses that had been plastered over in the Georgian period; the timber was re-exposed in the early part of the twentieth century. In 1901 it was known as the Vaults and it was owned by Allsopp's Brewery of Burton-on-Trent. At this time there were three bars, a smoke room, a market room and accommodation for travellers in seven bedrooms. The inn was renamed Ye Olde Bull Ring Tavern in the 1930s. To the left on the corner of Old Street was another inn, which has been variously known as the Bear and White Lion, the Imperial Vaults and the Prince Rupert, after Prince Rupert of the Rhine, a kinsman of Charles I who came to fight on the side of the Royalists during the Civil War. Today the corner section is a pleasant coffee house and restaurant called the Olive Branch.

Opposite, below: Adjacent to Ye Olde Bull Ring Tavern was another inn called the Bear. Like the Bull Ring it was housed in a fine timber-framed building from the late sixteenth to early seventeenth centuries. It was first listed as an inn in about 1635 and was in existence until 1810 when it was converted into a chemist's shop by George Woodhouse. In 1896 the shop was listed as an 'agricultural, family & dispensing chemist & druggist & seedsman, registered dentist & co.; depot for photographers' materials and chemicals; deputy registrar of births & deaths & vaccination officer for Ludlow sub-district'. The shop was taken over by Boots in the mid-1930s, and is now occupied by Jumpers, a ladies' clothes shop.

WAITING LIMITED TO 40 MINS IN ANY HOUR

Boots
DISPENSING CHEMISTS
WAITING LIMITED TO 40 MINS IN ANY HOUR
NO WAITING

Wainwright's shop was established in 1879 and was situated at 1 Bull Ring for so long that this area became known as Wainwright's Corner. He appears to have started off as a boot and shoemaker before becoming a saddler and extending his business into other types of leather goods. By 1960 the shop was also selling fancy goods and sports equipment, including fishing tackle, and was known as the Bull Ring Gift Shop (see opposite). Today it is the Teme Valley Antique and Jewellery Shop.

The shop with the large blinds is a branch of W.H. Smith, the newsagents, booksellers and stationers. As in so many other towns in the country the company's first appearance in Ludlow was as an outlet at the railway station, which opened in the 1880s. Smith's opened this branch in the town in about 1905 and the business remained there for a good part of the twentieth century. Today the company no longer has a shop in the town and the Staffordshire Building Society now uses the building.

Currys' stores were very popular in the 1960s, selling a wide range of electrical goods for the home at moderate prices and good hire purchase terms. In the summer of 1960 you could buy the latest transistor radios to listen to your favourite programmes while on holiday. Models varied from the tiny Perdio 'Piccadilly' pocket transistor costing 14½ guineas to the Ultra Transistor Six at 21 guineas; or on hire purchase terms of £1 deposit and thirty-eight payments of 9*s* 2*d*. Before Currys occupied the building it was Adney & Co., fancy drapers, and then a grocery shop run by Hunters the Teamen Ltd; today it is the Oxfam shop.

These next two photographs show the other end and side of the island of shops to the north of the Bull Ring, known as the Shelde (see page 37). Ross & Son acquired the business in about 1900 from E. Turner & Co., which was established in 1832. In the 1920s their slogan was 'Footwear For All People And All Purposes!' By 1960 they were specialising in high-grade exclusive footwear, selling Lotus, Clarks, Morland and Start-Rite shoes. They continued to repair boots and shoes at moderate prices and they also had the latest X-ray fitting service to measure your feet. The shop still deals in footwear but is now trading under the name of Peter Briggs.

For nearly a hundred years there was a sweet shop at 4 Bull Ring. It was started by William Cox, who was listed as a wholesale and retail confectioner in 1895, and was later run by Mrs Emily Cox. At the beginning of the 1930s the business was bought by G. Stuart-Page, who opened Stuart's Café here. In 1960 the café catered for morning coffee, luncheons and afternoon teas. Their homemade cakes were a speciality; they also sold a variety of confectionery and were agents for Fuller's Chocolates. The shop was later occupied by a stationer, but is now the premises of McKenzie & Smith, furniture restorers. The windows date from the early nineteenth century and are still an attractive feature of the shop.

In 1960 this building was a greengrocer, fruiterer and confectionery shop run by W.H. Penny. In the early part of the twentieth century the business was run by Philip Penny who was listed as a dairyman; he had taken it over from J. & J. Batty. In 1929 he was still running a dairy from this site but had also established a shop at Burway Cottage in Bromfield Road on the fringes of the town. The slogan of the shop in 1960 was 'Service That Satisfies'. The building now houses a gift shop called As You Like It.

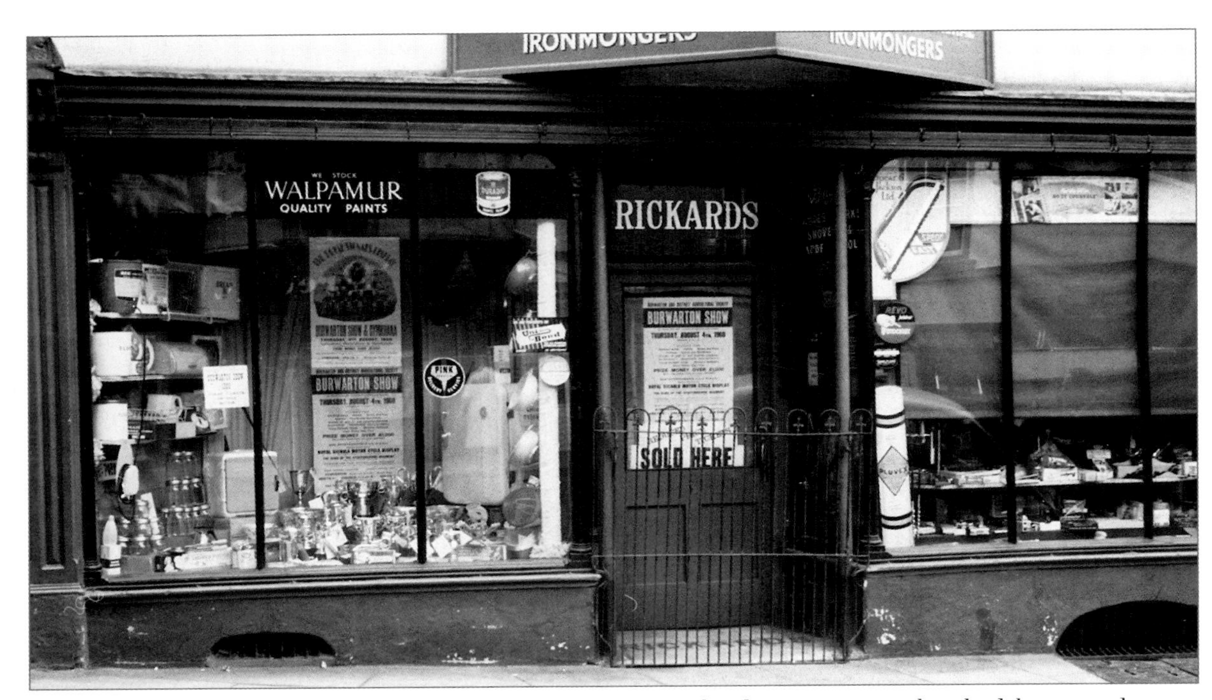

The firm of Rickards was established in 1864 by Heber Rickards in premises that had been used as an ironmongers since 1764. Part of the building was an inn known as the Salutation in the late seventeenth and early eighteenth centuries. In 1960 the shop sold a wide variety of ironmongery, as well as paint and everything for the garden. On display are forks at £3 8*s*, bone meal, compost maker and the Ladybird Lawnmower. Note the poster in the window advertising the Burwarton Show on Thursday 4 August and the display of the prizewinners' cups. Prize money was listed as £1,000 and top entertainment was provided by the Royal Signals Motor Cycle Display Team. Reduced price tickets could be obtained from the shop. Rickards' shop is still trading in the town and the frontage has changed very little over the years, with the front doors still protected by the neat little wrought-iron gates when the shop is shut.

George Davies had run a baker's shop from these premises since the 1870s. Other members of the family continued baking bread into the 1920s, when the shop was sold to the grocery firm of Melias. At this time the company had outlets in all the main market towns in the county. Note the poster advertising all blends of Horniman's Tea reduced to 8*d* per lb. From 1330 until the middle of the sixteenth century this site was occupied by a blacksmith's forge. Today the frontage has been taken back and the building incorporated into the HSBC bank next door.

The North & South Wales Bank opened a branch in Ludlow in about 1900. It was amalgamated with the London City & Midland Bank, which became known as the Midland Bank in 1908, the year this building was erected. It was built by the Ludlow building firm of Turford and Southward in a Tudor style that it thought would blend in with the architecture of Ludlow. Over the doorway are two dates, 1836 and 1905. The windows contain small panes of stained glass depicting medieval figures and coats of arms. The bank has now merged with HSBC.

Charles Jones traded as a pork and family butcher from these premises from the middle of the 1920s. It is still a butcher's shop today but now belongs to A.H. Griffith – 'Purveyors of Meat'. The frontage has been changed with the door into the shop being moved to the side under a covered area with another doorway leading to a flat above. Note the pigs carrying pork pies on trays on either side of Mr Jones's name.

Opposite, above: Nos 12 and 13 Bull Ring were known in the 1950s and '60s as the Ludlow Winter Garden. Joseph Price, a hairdresser, first occupied the buildings in about 1900. By 1917 he was also listed as a maker of wicker furniture with a works down in Lower Broad Street. In 1960 no. 12 was still a ladies' and gentlemen's hairdressers and a tobacconists selling Players and Churchman's cigarettes. Today the frontage has been greatly altered and is occupied by Nock Deighton, the estate agent. The café next door was opened in the 1930s and continued to operate until about 1968 when Eileen Gerrard's fashion shop moved there from King Street. In 1960 the café was open throughout the week and catered for individuals and private parties; the proprietor at this time was Gene Pacini. The frontage of this section has also changed but the steps are the same and the café is now occupied by Creative Lighting the lighting specialists.

COOKED MEAT SPECIALISTS
HAIRDRESSING
LADIES & GENTLEMENS
de Courcy Price
Phone-148.
WAITING LIMITED TO 40 MINS IN ANY HOUR
8 AM TO 8 PM
SENIOR SERVICE
Player's Please
TOBACCO
CAFE
WINTER GARD

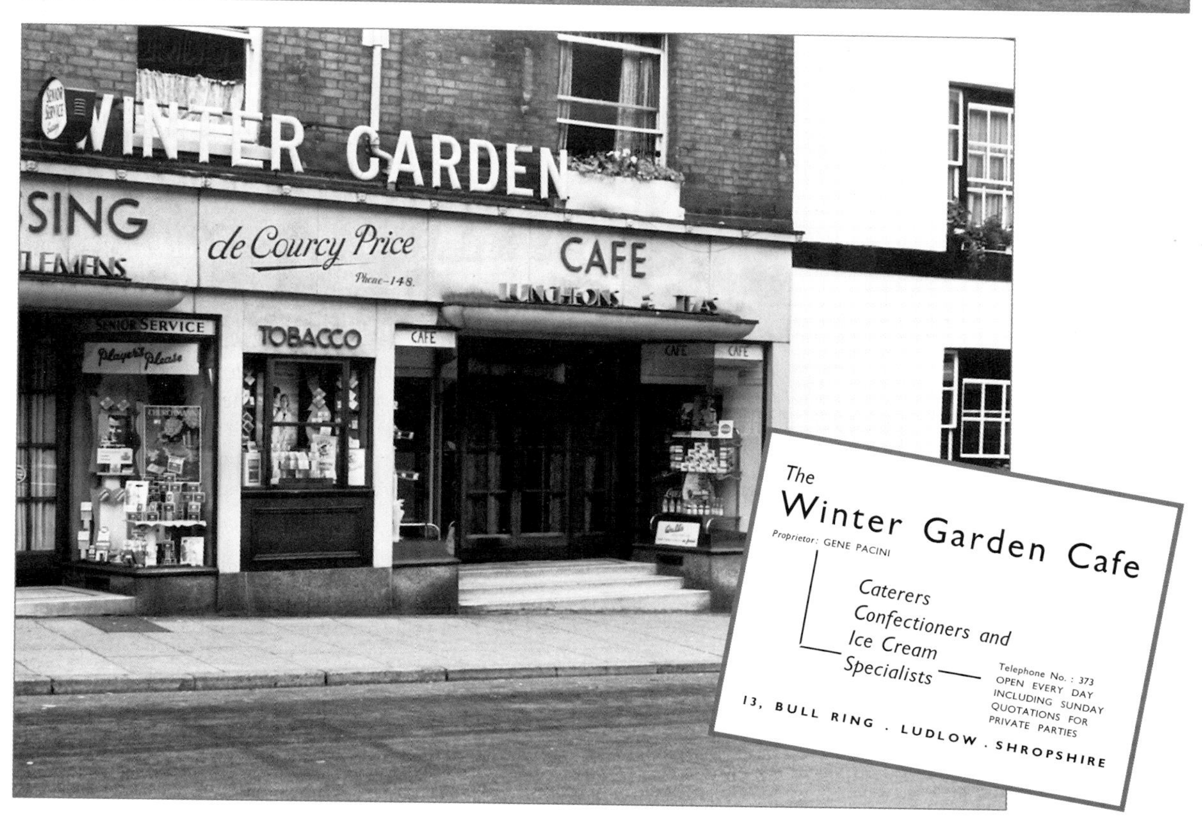
WINTER GARDEN
SSING
LEMENS
de Courcy Price
Phone-148.
CAFE
LUNCHEONS & TEAS
SENIOR SERVICE
Player's Please
TOBACCO
CAFE
The
Winter Garden Cafe
Proprietor: GENE PACINI
Caterers
Confectioners and
Ice Cream
Specialists
Telephone No.: 373
OPEN EVERY DAY
INCLUDING SUNDAY
QUOTATIONS FOR
PRIVATE PARTIES
13, BULL RING · LUDLOW · SHROPSHIRE

Parts of the Bull Hotel date back to the fourteenth century with several additions including a galleried range forming the yard at the rear, which was built in the fifteenth century when the building first became an inn. It was greatly damaged in 1693 by rioters who objected to a Presbyterian meeting being held there. The frontage was remodelled in the Georgian style after a fire in 1794 destroyed the front of the building.

This building was purpose built for the National Provincial Bank in 1924, its modern timber-frame designed to fit in with its surroundings. It stands on the site of a former inn called the Elephant and Castle. The NatWest Bank now conducts its business here. The only change to the frontage is that cash machines have been installed under the bay window.

This is the last building in the Bull Ring before you enter Corve Street. At one time J. & B. Blower Ltd of Shrewsbury occupied it. They were house furnishers and removal and storage agents, carpet warehousemen and funeral furnishers, with offices on Pride Hill and in Castle Gates. In 1960 it was known as Ceramics, and sold a variety of china, glass, toys and bric-à-brac. For a number of years now the building has housed Capitol Carpets, which advertised 'Pattern Selection, Fitted Perfection, In Any Direction'.

3

Tower Street, Upper Galdeford & Old Street

This is a view along Upper Galdeford looking towards Station Drive. All of the buildings on the left have been demolished to make way for a One-Stop convenience store, Somerfields supermarket and car park and the Portcullis Surgery. At one time this must have been a drinker's paradise as six of the buildings on that side of the road were public houses. In this view we can see the Three Horse Shoes and the Portcullis but at one time the building between them was the Dolphin. That inn closed in about 1900 and was converted into two shops. One of these became the Dolphin Café but was later converted into the Ludlow office of the Midland Red Bus Co.

This street's name recalls a tower next to the Galdeford gate, which was once used as a gaol but was removed in 1764. In 1891 Mrs Martha Davies was the owner of this tobacconist and confectionery shop. By 1937 Mrs Alice Davies was the shopkeeper and the premises were shared with Richard Davies, who was listed as a shipping engineer. By 1960 the business had changed hands and was being run by H.J. & R. Gilbey. Today it is the Old Cobblers Shop. The house to the right is still a private dwelling but the concrete has been removed from the front to reveal the brickwork.

The main Valeting Service dry cleaning laundry was in King Street. In the 1950s it was advertised as 'The distinctive drycleaners and dyers. The fastest service in the world, with branches everywhere'. By the 1960s competition was growing and just across the road at 12 Tower Street Ludlow's first laundrette was opened. It was called the Launderama and it offered a wash for 2*s* 6*d*, drying at 6*d* a load and up to 10lb of dry cleaning for just 10*s*. There was also a dry cleaning service available if required. Home Décor now occupies this shop. In 1921 the premises were occupied by John Fury, a hairdresser, who was in direct competition with William Wainwright, who ran a similar business from the house to the left.

Baxters had a number of butcher's shops around the county at this time. These premises had been used as a butcher's for several years and was once part of a large chain called the London Central Meat Co. Ltd, which had moved here in the 1920s from 67 Broad Street. It took over the Tower Street shop from George Watkins who was also a butcher. The premises are now occupied by Age Concern.

The shop in the centre was a baker's shop for many years. It was occupied in 1917 by Richard Wait & Sons, a baker and flour dealer who had started his business in the 1880s as a grocer at 101 Corve Street. By 1917 he was trading from 6 Tower Street, 77 Upper Galdeford and 70 Corve Street. By 1921 this shop was being run by Alfred Wait until a Mr Davies acquired the business. The Old Bakehouse Restaurant and Tea Shop now occupy the building.

The Shrewsbury Industrial Co-operative Society was founded in Shrewsbury towards the end of the nineteenth century. It opened a branch in Ludlow in the early years of the twentieth century at 22 Corve Street before moving to this purpose-built shop in about 1934. An inn called the Black Boy, which gave its name to a passage that ran to the side, once occupied part of the site. The building to the right is Ludlow Gaol, built in about 1764 for £422 on the site of the ancient Galdeford's Tower. To the right of the gaol in Upper Galdeford is the Advertiser Building.

Below: There were once four public houses side by side this short stretch of road. The shop on the left was the first recorded in 1744 and closed at the beginning of th nineteenth century. To the right are the Three Horse Sh the Dolphin and the Portcullis. Part of the Dolphin was occupied by the enquiry office of the 'Friendly Midland Red', which in 1960 was offering daily services to Shrewsbury, Hereford and Birmingham and to other m towns in the region. It also had on offer coach cruise holidays to a variety of destinations.

The Three Horse Shoes, Upper Galdeford. This building was first licensed in the eighteenth century and was selling beer until 1967 when the council purchased the site and the inn was demolished to make an access road into the new car park. Note the sign on the left advertising the 'Horse Shoes Garage, Motor Engineers, coach work, welding and spraying. Phone 435. Cars for Hire.' The shop next door, which was once part of the Dolphin, belonged to C.E. Bownes who was listed as an electrical contractor and sold a wide variety of electrical appliances.

An inn was first recorded on the site of the Portcullis in the eighteenth century, but it was knocked down towards the end of the Victorian era when this new building was erected to house it. It was the last of the four public houses on this stretch of road to remain open, pulling its last pint in about 1990. Across the road is the *Advertiser* building with two of the shops being occupied by J.P. Wood & Sons and Palmers boot and shoe repair and retailing shop. A plaque on the building reads 'Advertiser Buildings Erected By W.F. Marks A.D. 1914'.

Old Street looking towards the junction of Bull Ring and Tower Street. J.C. Lloyd's grocers was established at the end of the nineteenth century and seems to have its roots in the Shifnal area. During the first quarter of the twentieth century the firm opened a number of branches around the county and in the Wolverhampton area, coming to Ludlow in about 1925. By 1968 the grocer's had shut and Disc Bar Electronic Music Shop had opened there. At the moment the premises are occupied by Shapla Tandoori Restaurant and Take-away. Both Lloyd's premises and the building to the right were once a public house known as the Pheasant. It was first licensed in about 1800 and survived until just after the First World War. The lower building is now divided into two shops, with Stag Leisure Ware to the left and Allsorts household hardware to the right.

The origins of the West Midland Trustee Savings Bank date back to 1816 when the Abbey Savings Bank was founded in Shrewsbury. During the 1930s the bank expanded into several other towns with the Old Street branch opening in 1931. By the 1960s the bank had 4,539 open accounts with a balance of £1,066,542. At this time the manager was Mr Torrand. The motto for the bank was 'There is no safer or more convenient place for your savings than a Trustees Savings Bank'. In part of the building were the offices of Dyke & Ruscoe, incorporated accountants, who were also the secretaries of the Ludlow & District Chamber of Commerce. The building has now been adapted into flats with the ground floor being completely altered.

Behind this brick frontage on Old Street there are parts of a building dating back to the fifteenth century. In the seventeenth century it was an inn known as the Falcon, and later as the Red Lion. By the end of the 1920s G.H. Smallwood, an electrical engineer who had founded his business in Shrewsbury, opened this branch and another in Church Stretton. The business was still trading from here in the 1960s but today the premises are occupied by the Cat Protection League (Ludlow & District Branch).

Macdonald's Restaurant was ideally situated next to the Clifton cinema to cater for filmgoers either entering or leaving the cinema. It was open every day of the week from early morning until late in the evening and could supply you with breakfast, lunch, tea or a hot supper. The Evergreen Chinese Takeaway and fish and chip shop now occupy the building.

The Clifton was Ludlow's only purpose-built cinema, and was opened to the public for the first time in 1938. It was built on a site once occupied by Noakes's and Dean's Yards. It was converted into a bingo hall in the 1970s before being demolished in 1986 to make way for Clifton Court, sheltered accommodation for senior citizens.

Looking down Old Street towards Leominster. The first building on the left is now the Wonderland Chinese and English Food Take-away. The fencing below is in front of the British School, erected in 1895 and rebuilt in 1934. The school was used later as the headquarters for Ludlow Museum. Towards the bottom of the street on the left were three more inns; the Friars Inn, the Hen and Chickens (now both closed) and the Horse and Jockey at the foot of the bank. The timber-framed house on the right belonged to the Town Preacher and Lecturer; it was built in 1611. The garage and the building in which it was housed have gone and the new building on the site accommodates an antique shop.

James Evans established this business in 1851, although there had been drapers here since the seventeenth century. In the 1920s the business was taken over by R. Gordon Vooghts until Robert McMitchell acquired it. In 1960 it was described as the 'Fashion Centre of Ludlow', with shoppers being urged to 'Visit McMitchell's for Fashion, Fabrics and Gifts to suit all tastes'. It is now Mackays clothes shop. Sir William Jukes Steward, who went on to become the Speaker in New Zealand's House of Representatives, spent several years of his childhood in part of this building in the middle of the nineteenth century. It is easy to see why this part of King Street is known as the Narrows.

The Birmingham, Dudley & District Banking Co. Ltd opened a branch of their bank in Corve Street. The company later became known as the Birmingham District & Counties Banking Co. Ltd, and was backed by Williams Deacon & Manchester & Salford Bank Ltd, of London. It moved to this purpose-built bank in 1886. It later became part of Barclays Bank and is still trading from these premises today.

Below: This building was rebuilt in 1829. High up at the top of a downspout on the side of the house are the initials of Thomas Hotchkiss, a local saddle maker. In 1921 J. Evans & Son, which also had an outlet at 4 and 5 King Street, was using this shop. It was listed as general draper, milliner, costumier, ladies' underclothing and dressmaker. By 1929 Lennards' shoe shop had established itself in the building and traded there for over half a century. The Victoria Wine Shop now occupies the premises. Note the photographer at the corner of the shop who is taking a picture of the photographer!

This is the narrow approach leading to the south porch of the parish church of St Laurence. The porch was built in the Decorated style in the fourteenth century and was restored in 1860. It has a room above, which was used as a Deacon's Chamber before being set up as a library.

Sweetman's chemist's shop seems to be stuck in limbo between Church Street and King Street and its address is given in all the directories as The Cross, as it stands directly behind the Butter Cross. Robert Sweetman opened his shop here in about 1880, and as well as dispensing medicines he was an optician and sold a variety of photographic goods. By the 1960s the proprietor was Mr Mellings, who stocked many ladies' toiletries and was agent for Goya, Max Factor, Yardley, Coty and Fabergé products. Chris Williams, an estate agent, now occupies the premises.

To the left of Sweetman's chemist's shop is the Church Inn. The inn is reputed to date back to before the Reformation when it was known as the Cross Keys. Besides being an inn the building has been used for other purposes including a blacksmith's forge and by a barber-surgeon. The inn has also been known by a variety of names including the Wine Vaults, Wollaston's Wine Vaults, Exchange Vaults and the Gaiety from 1974 until 1979, when it took its present name.

College Street on the right takes its name from the college founded by the Palmers' Guild towards the end of the fourteenth century. The building over the arch and immediately joining it on the right is the Council Office. In 1960 it was used as Ludlow Museum, which has since been rehoused in the Assembly Rooms. The building on the left is the rear of the Butter Market while on the right is part of the Church Inn.

Valentine Dawes built the jettied building on the right and on a carved beam at the rear are his name and the date of the building, which was 1610. In the 1930s the building was the Headquarters of the Junior Imperial League (Ludlow Division). The Valentyne Dawes Gallery selling nineteenth-century antiques, paintings and furniture now occupies the shop. The Wrekin Ale sign is over the narrow entrance into the Rose & Crown. It is one of the town's oldest inns with parts of the building dating back to the fifteenth century.

The photographer is looking back from Castle Square towards Church Street on the left and Harp Lane on the right. The buildings that make these narrow lanes were built on the site of the rows of stalls occupied at one time by the butchers and shoemakers. Harp Lane takes its name from the Harp Inn, which once stood at the other end.

This is the narrow entrance to Church Street from Castle Square. In 1960 the building with the bay window on the first floor was the Conway Fish and Chip Restaurant. Today it is still a food outlet known as the Aragon Café, Restaurant and Takeaway. The frontage on the ground floor has been completely transformed. The name of the present restaurant takes its name from Catherine of Aragon, who spent a short time in the town after her marriage to Prince Arthur, the eldest son of Henry VII.

The Cross. Two columns at the entrance of the Butter Market are on the right and to the left of Wood's Shop is the High Street. Between Wood's and the Co-op is Harp Lane. Just visible is part of the building that housed the Harp Inn. There were inns of this name in the town and this one was recorded from the early eighteenth century until the 1870s.

Above: The timber-framed building to the left of the Butter Cross is called Tamberlaine House and was named after Tamberlaine Davies, a wealthy mercer who died in 1685. At the time of his death the stock in his shop was valued at £527 1s 9*d*, a vast amount at that time. The building was erected in the seventeenth century and has some nice carvings at the front and rear. There was another branch of the Co-op in Tower Street in 1960.

William Baker of Audlum in Cheshire designed the Butter Cross in 1743 on the site of the High Cross. M.E. Bodenham, a house furnisher, used part of the building. In 1929 the company was listed as 'complete house furnishers, undertakers & removal & storage contractors'. A jeweller, goldsmith and diamond merchant called Benson now occupies the shop.

King Street from the Bull Ring to the junction of the Butter Cross and Broad Street. The wonderful timber-framed building leaning out into the street is the clothes shop belonging to F. Bodenham, which has occupied that corner for around a century. Most of the properties on the left were once owned by the Palmers' Guild and were later transferred to the corporation. With the exception of the building with the dormer windows, which was erected in the nineteenth century, the rest have a timber-framed core behind a later frontage. Note the milk-dispensing machine on the right where you could obtain a carton of milk, a strawberry milk shake or a carton of orange juice for just 6*d*.

Bodenham's shop occupies the whole corner at the junction of King Street and Broad Street. The company has been trading in Ludlow since the middle of the nineteenth century and was recorded in *Cassey's Directory* for 1871 as drapers and hosiers trading from King Street and the Narrows. Note the posters in the doorway advertising a pony show and gymkhana, Ludlow flag day, the opening of Henley Hall Gardens and the carnival and sports day to be held on August Bank Holiday Monday.

The timber-framed building dates from the very early fifteenth century and was once divided into four shops with living accommodation on the upper floors. The Butter Cross on the right was erected in 1743 and cost in the region of £1,000. The ground floor was used for the sale of butter and other dairy produce while the Blue Coat Charity School, which reopened there with forty-five pupils in 1785, used the top floor. At the end of the nineteenth century the Revd E. Clayton and other local clergymen opened a Workingmen's Evening Club there.

Eileen Gerrard's shop sold good quality ladies' wear including gowns, costumes, mantles, knitwear and hosiery in all the well-known makes. The proprietors in 1960 were D.A. and E.C. Falshaw and among their stock was a full-length royal blue corded evening dress by Elmoor costing £8 18*s* 6*d* and a blue chiffon nylon short evening dress by Linzi, which had a gathered skirt with two underskirts, one of taffeta and one of net. The price, complete with matching stole, was 11 guineas. By 1968 the shop had moved to 13 Bull Ring.

Until the middle of the 1930s Bodenhams had another draper's shop at 18 and 19 King Street, which was later split into International Stores, listed in 1937 as provision merchants, and Eileen Gerrard's ladies' shop. The building they occupied was built in the nineteenth century and was called 'the ugliest in Ludlow' by TV historian Alec Clifton-Taylor. In recent years the building has been converted back into one unit and is now occupied by a clothing shop called Seconds Ahead.

The Regent Cycle Works that was owned by H.E. Bryan and A. Handy once occupied this shop. They moved there in about 1918. By the 1930s they had expanded their business by opening a radio store as well as continuing to be cycle agents. By 1960 the Quality Cleaners had moved in and were advertising cheap rates for freshening holiday garments, an eighteen-hour quality service and boiler suits cleaned for 1*s* 6*d*. Just three doors to the left were their big rivals, the Valeting Service Dry Cleaning Co. The frontage has been altered in recent years and the shop now lies empty.

For most of the first half of the twentieth century the shop in the centre was a tobacconist belonging to T. and E. Bradley. By 1960 it had become Smith's sports and gift shop. An advert from that date urged visitors: 'Don't forget to take a gift from the Gift & Sports Shop. Crested souvenirs, games, fishing tackle, camping equipment, everything for swimmers, sporting guns. Smiths Sport Shop King Street.' The shop is now occupied by Birthdays, selling a variety of cards and confectionery – including delicious Thornton's chocolates.

MAYPOLE
MAYPOLE
VALETING SERVICE CLEANERS
THE TWO 2/3
MAYPOLE DAIRY CO LT

IMPERIAL WALLPAPER Co
DYERS VAL
DURADIO
DURADIO

Wilfred Tay's family butcher's shop was housed in these premises for many years. In 1960 it was advertised as purveyors of prime English meat and were noted for their Welsh mutton and speciality sausages. The small sign over the door informs customers that Ella C. Tay was licensed to sell game. The shop is now occupied by Cancer Research UK.

Opposite, above: The Maypole moved into this shop in about 1920, but before that it was occupied by John Bishop, a tanner, currier, leather and grindery merchant. The business was established in 1709 and the tannery was situated in Corve Street. By 1917 his executors were running the grindery business from these premises. The Maypole was a countrywide grocery business with several branches in Shropshire. Their window is full of marvellous offers including jam at 2*s* 3*d* a jar, salad cream at 1*s* a bottle and on special offer 1lb of lard and 2lb of sugar at 2*s* for both. Today the Cotswold Collection occupies the shop.

Opposite, below: The Imperial Wallpaper Co. occupy a shop that once belonged to Thomas Micklewright, who was listed as an art cabinet maker, upholsterer, complete house furnisher, dealer in antiquities and funeral director. Micklewright's was established in 1870 and remained in these premises into the twentieth century. In 1960 the wallpaper shop was selling a vast range of wallpaper priced between 2*s* 9*d* and 8*s* 4*d* a roll. Today the shop has gone back to selling furniture and operates under the name of Pineland. The alley to the left is called Fish Street.

Here the photographer is standing in King Street looking towards the Bull Ring. In 1960 the last building in the Bull Ring and part of the first one in King Street housed the business of Keysell & Co. Ltd. In 1905 its advertisement claimed it was established in 1780 and was a wine merchant, agent for Bass & Alsopp's Burton Ales, Guinness's celebrated Dublin stouts, Pale Ale and Schweppes's mineral waters. It also sold Keysell's Old Liquor Scotch Whisky a full-cream Highland whisky, guaranteed fifteen years old and costing 48*s* a dozen. Prospective buyers could have a free sample on application! The Bull Ring premises are now used by the travel agent Lunn Poly while Bank's confectionery shop is a ladies' clothes shop called Bubbles.

5

Broad Street

Broad Street was described by Nikolaus Pevsner as 'one of the most memorable streets in England. It is wide with pavements raised by cobbled inclines.' In 1960 the cobbles on the left-hand side were covered with tarmac, which caused an indignant outcry. They were restored and are now listed. The steep incline leads down to the Broad Gate, the last of five main gateways into town. Halfway down the street two roads feed into Broad Street: on the right below the large white building is Bell Lane and on the left below the timber-framed building is Brand Lane.

This is a good view of the narrow Broad Gate leading through to Lower Broad Street. The gatehouse has a medieval core with later additions, the Gothic battlements having been added in the eighteenth century. The entrance to Brand Lane is on the left and the house just below the sign, half white and half grey, was a public house called the Star Inn. Further down the bank on the same side was another inn called the Anchor. The fine-looking house with the long rounded window over the door was built in 1685 for Sir Job Charlton and was renovated in 1764.

In the eighteenth century the timber-framed building on the corner of Brand Lane was an inn called the Peacock. In the early part of the twentieth century most of the buildings in this area were private homes. A Mrs Dawes lived just above the half-timbered house at no. 21 in 1937 while in the houses to the left lived the Baker and Barnett families. The old Peacock Inn is now a video hire shop. Brand Lane has in the past been called either Burnt or Brant Lane.

The narrow house on the right with steps at the front door was erected in 1738 while the one to the left was built a year earlier as the town house of the Salways from Richard's Castle; they were strong Parliamentarians and supporters of the Whig Party. In the nineteenth century it was the premises of the Salop Old Bank owned by Eyton, Burton, Lloyd & Co. The house is now occupied by Green the solicitors and by Broad Street Books.

Before moving to this purpose-built building, Lloyd's Bank was situated in Castle Square and was known as Lloyds, Barnett & Bosanquets Bank Ltd, with the manager in 1885 being Charles Pickering. Over a hundred years later the bank still trades from these premises but has amalgamated with the Trustees Savings Bank in Old Street. The frontage to the building on the right was erected at the beginning of the eighteenth century, but there is an older timber-framed section at the rear. The building is now occupied by R.G. Cave & Sons which sell fine quality antiques.

The building that houses the Wool Shop was erected at the beginning of the seventeenth century. For a short while it was the home of William Owen, who became the portrait painter of the Prince Regent. For a number of years it was known as a Fancy Repository, a shop that would have sold a great variety of goods including wool and other haberdashery. It became known as the Wool Shop in the middle of the last century. In 1960 it advertised 'a remarkable display of wools for a county town and a centre of intense interest for visitors. Here you will find a fine range of wools from the mills of Britain and France. We post many parcels to the Commonwealth and the USA. This is a personal service shop.' The proprietor at this time was Mrs H.J. Pearce.

The shop between the two timber-framed buildings was built in about 1439 and is thought to have been an inn. In 1885 it was occupied by William Sharp, a hairdresser and photographer, who advertised that hot and cold shower baths were always available at his shop. In about 1900 Thomas Raulins opened his music warehouse here, selling a variety of instruments including organs, pianos and harmoniums, and also sheet music. The business had been established in 1854 by W.A. Boucher at 21 Broad Street, where Mr Raulins had worked as his manager. By 1960 the firm had started to sell electrical items such as radios and record players, and televisions made by Ekco, Bush and Ferguson.

The first mention of the Angel Hotel was in 1551 and unlike other hostelries it retained that name throughout its history. It was one of the town's principal coaching inns, with its most famous coach, the *Aurora*, making the journey from Ludlow to London in just twenty-seven hours in the early 1820s. In 1802 Lord Nelson addressed a crowd from one of the bow windows, while staying at the inn with his mistress Emma and her husband Sir William Hamilton. Napoleon's brother Lucien Bonaparte is reputed to have dined there while a prisoner of war in Ludlow in 1814. In about 1900 accommodation at the hotel consisted of a bar and parlours, a coffee room, a billiards room and eighteen bedrooms, with stabling at the rear for eleven horses.

The shop behind the car and bus belongs to E.J. Poyner, a children's outfitter and general draper. He moved into the upper section of the shop in about 1920, next door to Frank Daulby, another draper; both were selling side by side until Poyner's finally took over the other business. The shop still trades under the name of E.J. Poyner today.

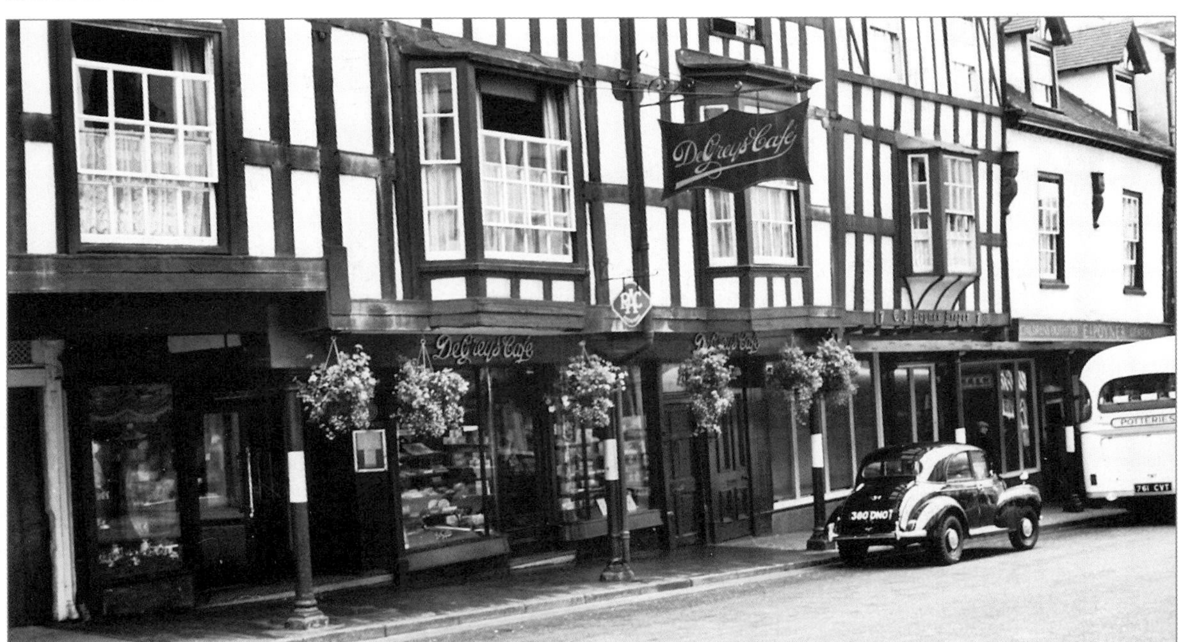

In the late sixteenth and early seventeenth centuries De Greys Café was an inn called the Swann. In 1900 the premises were occupied by Herbert Smith, a 'fashionable boot and shoemaker' and agent for the 'celebrated K boots and shoes'. His shop was taken over by the National Boot and Shoe Co.'s Freeman, Hardy and Willis chain until it moved to the corner of Tower Street and the Bull Ring in the 1920s. De Greys opened here shortly afterwards and became quite an institution in the town, being advertised as 'One of the larger and finer café-restaurants in the Midlands'. They were also listed as confectioners, pastrycooks and chocolate manufacturers.

Parts of the building above De Greys have been dated to the middle of the fourteenth century. In 1960 Valentine's grocery shop was still open but had disappeared by the end of the decade. It was established in 1757 and was described in 1917 as a 'family grocer & provision dealer & tea & coffee merchant; agent for W. & A. Gilbey Ltd, wine & spirit merchants'. They also had another branch in Craven Arms and were agents for the Royal Exchange (Fire & Life) Insurance Co. and the Plate Glass Insurance Co. The building was owned in the twentieth century by Joseph Burton & Son Ltd.

Until the erection of the building to the left of Valentine's store, the shop marked the top of Broad Street on the eastern side. Note the cast-iron pillars supporting the upper storeys to create a covered way. It extends downhill as far as no. 10 and has been compared to an Italian piazza or the Rows at Chester. Just to the right of the shop is an alleyway that has been opened to the public in recent years. It connects Broad Street to Old Street and is called Valentine's Walk.

The photographer is standing in the High Street looking towards McMitchell's shop in King Street. The magnificent timber-framed building was built at the beginning of the seventeenth century, narrowing the junction quite considerably at the top of Broad Street. Bodenhams moved its business to these premises in about 1900. Before that it had been trading in King Street.

The large white building is Oriel House. It stands on the site of the Talbot Inn, recorded from the late fifteenth until the middle of the seventeenth century. Talbot was the family name of the Earls of Shrewsbury who owned the property. At other times it was also called the Antelope or the Rayndeer. By the 1930s Oriel House was occupied by George Hide, while William Farmer JP lived next door. In 1960 the buildings were being used as the Tally Ho Hotel and by an antique dealer.

This building is now a private house but in the 1840s it was a post office. It was later the home and studio for Walter Harper, a children's photographer and an expert in animal, commercial and landscape photography. By 1960 it was a gift shop whose proprietors urged people who were shopping in Ludlow to 'Visit the Gift Shop. Where you will find a choice of unusual and lovely gifts, also many things you will want yourself. We are local stockists for Wedgwood and Royal Worcester. Gifts, china, novelties, souvenirs, picture-frames & toys. Printed stationery of all kinds.' Note the poster advertising Shrewsbury Flower Show to the left of the door.

An inn known as the Falcon stood on this site, but it was removed in about 1743 when a new house designed by William Baker was erected for Richard Salwey. This house also became an inn, known as the Crown, but after a visit by a young Princess Victoria it was renamed the Royal Kent, Victoria & Crown. It closed in 1848 and became a private residence until it was demolished to make way for a new Wesleyan chapel in 1879. The new chapel was built in the Italianate style and made of brick with a stone dressing. It cost about £5,000.

In the 1970s the owners of this fine timber-framed house were surprised to find that behind the seventeenth-century frontage and hidden by many years of internal DIY was an almost complete two-bay medieval hall. For many years part of the ground floor was used as a dental surgery. The patients' waiting room was to the right of the front door and on the chimney breast of that room behind a carved panel is a fine coat-of-arms, which incorporates the arms of James I.

Augustus Roberts opened his ironmonger's shop at 55 Broad Street in the 1920s. Until then the shop had been occupied by Edward Robinson, an earthenware dealer. The left-hand section of Mr Roberts' shop (above) had been the Swan & Falcon in the middle of the eighteenth century while at the same time the building to the left had also been a public house known as the White Hart. A third public house, the Crown, occupied the upper section of the ironmonger's shop (below) and the building next door (the gas showroom on the next page). It was one of Ludlow's largest and most fashionable inns until the owner went bankrupt in 1818 and the name was transferred to another inn further down the road. In 1960, as well as supplying his customers with a full range of ironmongery, Mr Roberts also supplied all their garden needs and kept a full range of wallpaper and paint for home decoration.

In the late nineteenth and early twentieth centuries this was the depot of the Society for Promoting Christian Knowledge. It was acquired in the 1920s as a showroom by the Ludlow Union Gas Co. Ltd, the offices of which were across the road at no. 14 and gas works were at Temeside. In 1960 it offered a number of labour-saving appliances including the 'silent gas fridge'. It was supposed to keep your food fresh and make mid-week shopping easier and cheaper, and to keep your perishable food safe from flies and contamination. The advert ended with these words in bold black type: 'Gas Saves Food Waste'. The Shapla Restaurant now occupies the premises.

This property was once part of Bodenham & Sons who were house furnishers, storage and removal specialists, as well as being drapers. Astons was a house furnisher and furniture manufacturer. It had a number of other stores around the county and moved here in the 1930s. In 1960 it held a special kitchen and linoleum event, which was full of outstanding bargains. You could purchase a 2ft 6in wide kitchen cabinet, finished in enamel in a variety of colours, with a wooden worktable for just £10 15*s*. Printed cork linoleum, which was very fashionable, could be bought for 6*s* 11*d* per square yard. The Factory Shop, selling a range of bedding, towels, curtains and clothing, now occupies the building.

From the 1880s until the middle of the last century this building was occupied by a watchmaker and jeweller, first by Edward Robinson, who was also an earthenware dealer, at no. 55 and then by his son Geoffrey. G.A. Morris, a pork butcher, traded from there for several years, but today the premises are occupied by a firm called Broad Bean that sells wholefoods.

This shop was once occupied by the London Central Meat Co. Ltd until it moved to Tower Street, and then by Lucie Poole as a ladies' outfitters shop. By 1960 it was known as 'Myladi, where ladies shop'. The firm also had branches in Bridgnorth and Wellington. In 1960 the *Advertiser* reported that Myladi displayed 'a remarkable collection of suits in pebble tweeds and velours at five and a half and six and a half guineas, while their range of corsetry included models for every figure at prices from 16s 3d'. The shop now sells men's wear and is known as James & Co.

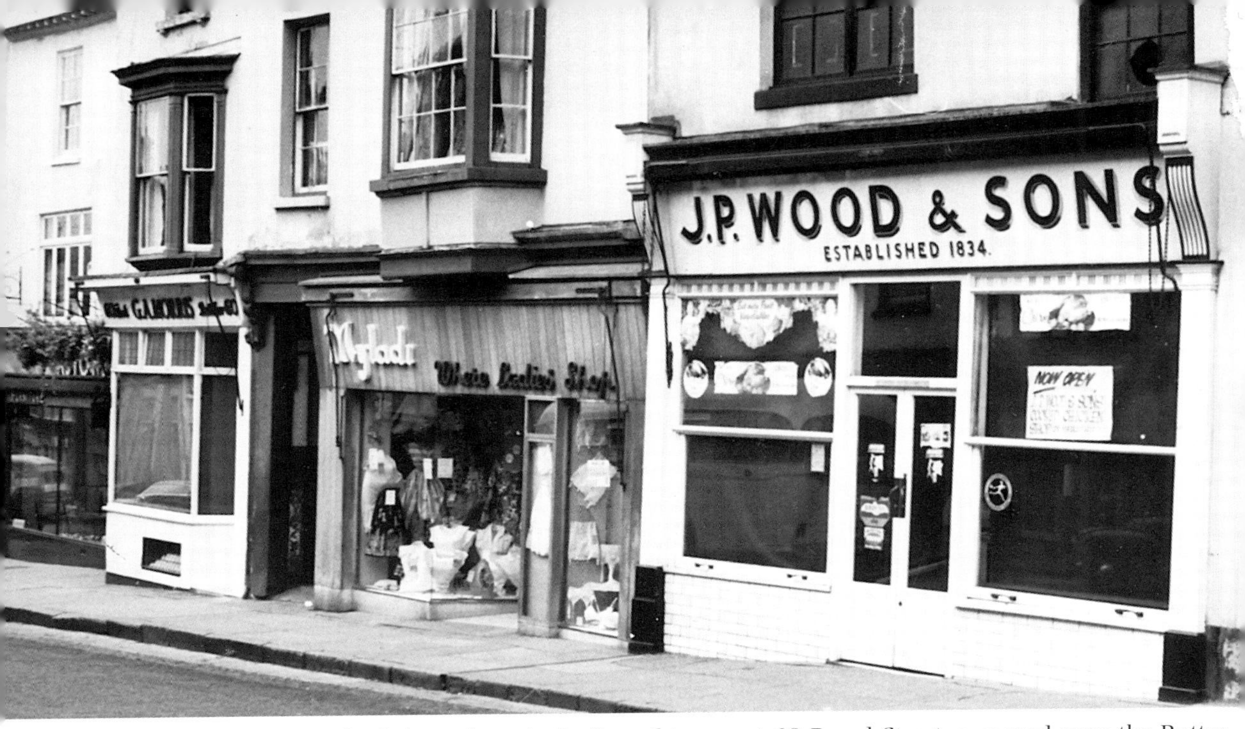

In 1960 J.P. Wood & Sons had three shops in Ludlow, this one at 68 Broad Street, a second near the Butter Cross and a third in Market Street. The firm originated from Market Street in Craven Arms and was established by J.P. Wood's father-in-law, James Overton. The firm expanded and was known nationally for the 'Chuckie Chicken' brand name. A poster in the window informs customers that their new cooked chicken shop had opened in Market Street. Dewhurst's butcher's shop is the last shop in Broad Street and stands on the corner of Market Street. It is a national firm and had several branches around Shropshire. It acquired this shop from the British & Argentine Meat Co. (1923) Ltd. In recent years both properties have been converted into one shop, which is now occupied by the Silver Pear and sells a wide variety of gifts and fancy goods.

6

Market Street & High Street

The narrow entrance to Market Street is on the left with the High Street to the right. At one time the High Street occupied the whole area, but in the thirteenth century a row of market stalls known as Baron's Row was eventually built over, creating the two separate streets. Market Street has also been known as Hand and Bell Lane and as Crown Back Lane. Unlike most streets in the town only one inn, the George, has been recorded in the High Street.

This view looks back along the High Street towards Bodenhams in Broad Street. All the buildings on the right were erected on Baron's Row. In the past the annual fairs and weekly town markets would have taken place in and around this area.

Opposite, above: Before Hepworths moved into this shop in the 1930s it was occupied in about 1900 by E.W. & W. Phillips who were tailors and had another shop in Shrewsbury. Another tailor, Edgar Lethbridge, traded there in the early 1900s and was listed as a 'ladies and gents tailor, breeches maker, motorists' outfitter, hatter and hosier'. The business was later run by W.A. Stimson Ltd. A group of Nonconformists once used part of the site for worship until they were driven out by a mob in 1731. They later built a chapel at the bottom of Corve Street. Today the building is occupied by McCartney's, a firm of estate agents and auctioneers of fine art and of livestock.

Opposite, below: For a short while at the beginning of the twentieth century this café was listed as refreshment rooms run by Edgar Sanders. In about 1905 Edward Philpott opened a fruit and wholesale and retail confectionery shop here. He also ran another fruit shop at 15 High Street that was established by his father William, but after a few years that was closed and he stopped selling fruit to concentrate on the confectionery side of his business. The Holly Bush provided visitors with a wide variety of light refreshments and snacks, Midland Counties ice cream, tea, coffee, milk shakes and mugs of hot Horlicks. Note the adverts on the window for Woodbine, Players, Senior Service and Craven 'A' cigarettes.

HEPWORTHS
HOLLYBUSH
Craven 'A'
High Class

HOLLYBUSH MILK BAR
Player's Please
Senior Service
Craven 'A'
HORLICKS
OPEN
HORLICKS
WOODBINE
A SNACK
MEAT

Carpenter's has been a butcher's shop for about a hundred years. The business was started by Richard Carpenter in Castle Square but he had moved to these premises by 1905. Before that Benjamin Raymond, a tailor and hatter, occupied the shop. Today the shop front remains unaltered by time and the width of the front still corresponds to the original medieval building; it is exactly 11ft wide. The business is continued by D.W. Wall & Son.

The shop on the left next to the butcher was split into two units in 1960. The left-hand section was a record shop called Disc Bar Electronics that also sold televisions, radios and record players, while the right-hand section was occupied by Davies's toyshop. The shop in the middle was occupied by Rowena Rawlings's confectionery shop. The building also housed the Ludlow Central Enquiry Office and Bodenham's Travel Agency. At this time it was a member of ABTA, agents for BEA and was able to arrange every form of business and holiday travel. It also organised car and coach hire, accommodation, theatre tickets, British and continental rail travel, foreign exchange and travellers cheques. Laver's confectionery occupied this shop for over half a century. Before that it was the Singer sewing machine shop, while at present it is occupied by Austin & Fawkes Interiors.

Benjamin Williams opened a shop in this building in the 1880s. He was listed as a 'linen & woollen draper, silk mercer, hosier & haberdasher'. He also sold mourning attire and was an undertaker. For a short while he had another outlet further down the street at no. 13 but was trading in this shop up to the middle of the last century. By 1960 the shop was being run by B. Williams, selling ladies', gents' and children's clothes. In their summer sale ladies' dresses were selling for 35*s*, although a sign in the window warns bargain hunters that goods marked sale price were for cash only.

Mr Williams also advertised that his prices were very competitive and that he stocked a large selection of household goods. Now the smaller section with the bay window on the second storey is Victoria Prints, while the double-fronted section is divided into two shops. The left-hand unit is now Outback which sells classical and jazz recordings, and on the right is Global World Gifts which advertises that it is 'importing the unusual'.

The Steward brothers opened a grocery and provisions shop in these premises towards the end of the nineteenth century. They had another shop on Pride Hill in Shrewsbury, and the son of one of the brothers had the distinction of being mayor of Shrewsbury throughout the Second World War. Today it is a shoe shop called Moshula, but in 1960 it was still a grocery and provisions shop run by W.S. Stephens, who had other outlets in Castle Street and Tower Street.

Below: James and Edward Harding opened a draper's and milliner's shop in these premises in the middle of the nineteenth century and traded there for over fifty years until the shop was occupied by Bradley's, the outfitters, which was later taken over by Foster Bros. At one period in its history the building had been used as an inn called the George, which was recorded from the middle of the sixteenth until the eighteenth century. Parts of the building date back to medieval times and when it was renovated in 1979 a large section of timber framing was uncovered.

The photographer is standing in Castle Street looking towards Market Street and Raven Lane. Bradley's outfitters is on the left and Woolworth's store is on the right. Matthews butcher's shop was once an inn called the Old Red Lion, and was there from the eighteenth to the middle of the nineteenth century. The section on the corner has been a butcher's shop for many years and is now occupied by Reg Martin & Sons, which sells an amazing variety of produce. The shop on the left is now occupied by Chichi of Ludlow which sells designer lingerie, swimwear, hosiery and gifts. Raven Lane takes its name from a large inn that stood halfway down the bank.

This view show the narrowness of Market Street, which is little more than a lane, created when the buildings on the left were built on the site of a row of stalls on the market place. Many of the buildings on the right were refronted over the years but most have an earlier timber-framed core. Five public houses have been recorded in the street but the only one still in operation in 2003 was the Globe Inn on the right. It was also known as the Red Lion and was first recorded in the eighteenth century.

This is the other corner of High Street looking down towards The Cross and Broad Street. Note the tower of St Laurence's Church peeping over the rooftops. The buildings on this side of the street were also built on the site of a row of market stalls. At the beginning of the twentieth century this shop was occupied by Francis Bell, a clothier and outfitter. The business was later taken over by the Midland Clothing Co., which was owned by Southern Brothers. The brothers also had another shop in Shrewsbury and in time both premises became known as Southern's Store. By 1960 the building was occupied by Collins Shoe Shop which advertised a new brand of 'K' shoes, 'Fulfit, made to slim the wider foot, comfortably cushioned on soft tread inner soles and like all "K" shoes they fit beautifully.' Rayner Optician Ltd now occupies the shop.

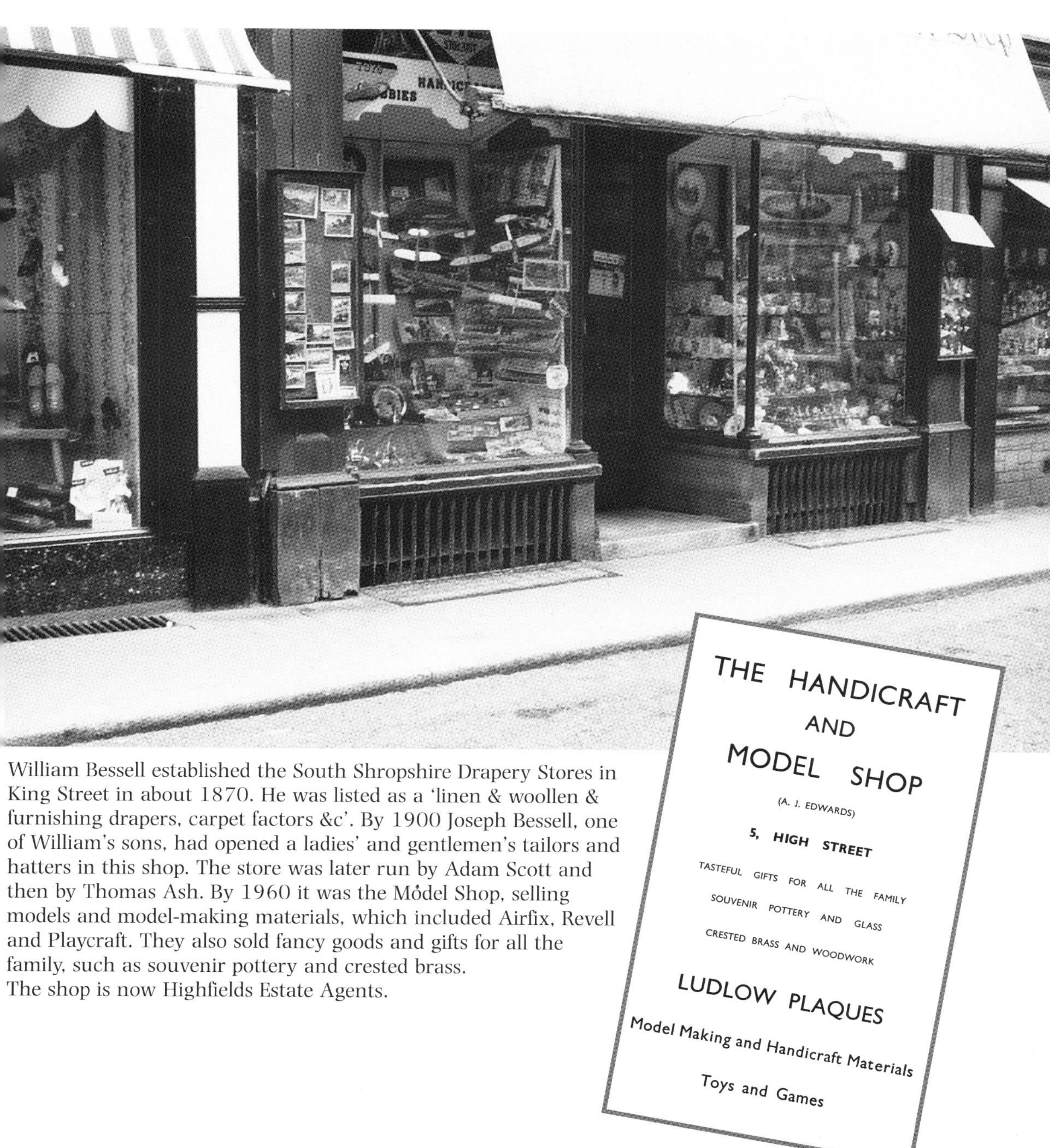

THE HANDICRAFT
AND
MODEL SHOP

(A. J. EDWARDS)

5, HIGH STREET

TASTEFUL GIFTS FOR ALL THE FAMILY
SOUVENIR POTTERY AND GLASS
CRESTED BRASS AND WOODWORK

LUDLOW PLAQUES

Model Making and Handicraft Materials

Toys and Games

William Bessell established the South Shropshire Drapery Stores in King Street in about 1870. He was listed as a 'linen & woollen & furnishing drapers, carpet factors &c'. By 1900 Joseph Bessell, one of William's sons, had opened a ladies' and gentlemen's tailors and hatters in this shop. The store was later run by Adam Scott and then by Thomas Ash. By 1960 it was the Model Shop, selling models and model-making materials, which included Airfix, Revell and Playcraft. They also sold fancy goods and gifts for all the family, such as souvenir pottery and crested brass.
The shop is now Highfields Estate Agents.

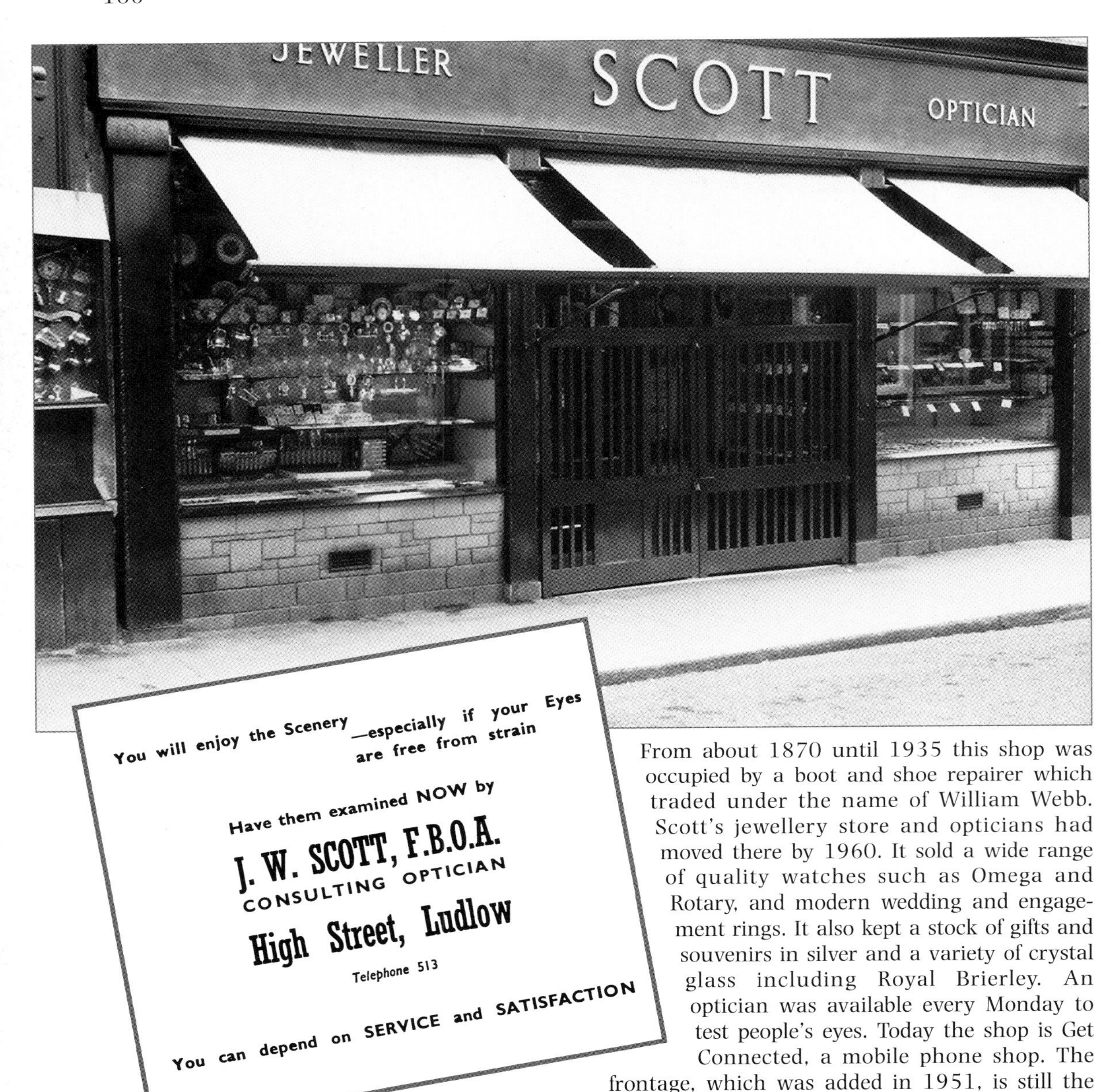

From about 1870 until 1935 this shop was occupied by a boot and shoe repairer which traded under the name of William Webb. Scott's jewellery store and opticians had moved there by 1960. It sold a wide range of quality watches such as Omega and Rotary, and modern wedding and engagement rings. It also kept a stock of gifts and souvenirs in silver and a variety of crystal glass including Royal Brierley. An optician was available every Monday to test people's eyes. Today the shop is Get Connected, a mobile phone shop. The frontage, which was added in 1951, is still the same. Note the date to the left of the window.

Opposite, below: This shop is also housed in a timber-framed building from the seventeenth century. In about 1900 Charles Cobbin, a bookseller, newsagent and stationer, had a shop here until he was taken over by Thomas Price who also owned the Electric Printing Works in the Bull Ring. Throughout the middle of the twentieth century the Grant family ran a fancy goods shop here before it became a newsagent again by 1960. Note the adverts for cigarettes and tobacco, which would not be allowed today. Along with the shop seen above this is now part of View ladieswear.

Behind the modern shop front and the brick façade lies a building that dates back to 1651. In 1900 John Harper, a hairdresser and umbrella maker, had his shop here, but four years earlier he ran his business from 7 Church Street. In the 1920s Lizzie Tomlinson had a confectionery shop here, and from 1929 the premises was occupied by Daniel Slack, a men's outfitter. The shop is now called View and sells ladies' clothes.

This four-storey building in the High Street was built in the middle of the seventeenth century with the Regency-style bow window a later addition. The main part of the shop with the awning has been rebuilt in recent times and the white brick to the left has been removed. Arthur Bessell, a wholesale and retail glass, china and earthenware dealer, traded from this shop in 1900. He also hired out crockery and glasses for large functions in the area. George Pearce, a fishmonger who also traded in fresh fruit and game, later acquired the shop. By 1960 J.P. Wood & Sons of Craven Arms had bought the business, which became one of its three shops in the town. In 1960 it was advertising that it had never known such an abundance of produce at such reasonable prices at this season of the year. New King Edward potatoes cost 2*s* for 3lb, frozen salmon 7*s* 6*d* per lb, grapes 2*s* 6*d* a bunch and daffodils 5*d* a bunch. It also advertised that wreaths, crosses, sprays and wedding bouquets could be supplied by its expert florists at short notice. The shop is now occupied by Osbourne Kelland Ladies' Wear.

7

Castle Street & Castle Square

The people of Ludlow were very proud of their new town hall when it was built in 1887. In *Kelly's Directory* of 1891 it was described as a 'handsome building of red brick and Bath stone dressing, in the Renaissance style'. The ivy-covered building was once known as the Castle Vaults Inn. It was removed recently and a block of town apartments, which blend in well with the older buildings, has been built on the site.

The George Hotel has stood on this site on Castle Street since the eighteenth century. In 1900 it consisted of a large bar, a sitting room, clubroom, two kitchens, eight bedrooms and stabling for twenty horses. In 1896 the landlady was taken to court and charged with diluting the whisky. She was found guilty and fined £1 10*s* plus costs of 1 guinea for analysing the liquor. The hotel is still open but now stands on a corner since a road was put through on the left to the car park.

In the distance is Ludlow's famous castle, on the left is the market hall and on the right the George Hotel. In the early part of the twentieth century the house in the distance on the right with the pillars at the front door belonged to Mrs Mary Partridge, who let out apartments. Now the ground floor is a shop called the Chocolate Gourmet while the upper floors have been turned into flats. The writing on the wall just to the right of the George is advertising baths, sinks and sanitary fittings for one of Price's ironmonger's shops.

This is an excellent view of the north side of the town and market hall. The hall was built in 1887 to commemorate the Diamond Jubilee of Queen Victoria. Note the plaque with the date and the coat-of-arms on the right of the oriel window. It was built on the site of the old market hall, which had been erected in 1702.

This building was also a public house, known as the Sun Inn. It was open from the middle of the eighteenth to the middle of the nineteenth century. Thomas Rider, a pork butcher, traded from this shop in the early part of the twentieth century. By 1929 Mrs Pyle had opened a fried fish restaurant here and she was followed by Walter Edison, listed as a fried fish dealer. William Price started as a plumber in Raven Lane before moving to 4 Castle Street, a few doors to the right, where he continued as a plumber as well as opening an ironmonger's shop. By 1960 he was also trading from this shop at 10 Castle Street. Today the building is part of Kwik Save's supermarket.

Jeffery Cornelius Austen opened a printing works in Broad Street in about 1900. He was listed as a 'Bookseller, fancy stationer, printer, book binder, newsagent, public library and insurance agents'. The company moved to these premises in the 1920s. Before becoming a printing works the building was used as the town's main post office, and this area of Castle Street was known for a time as Post Office Square. In 1960 a jeweller occupied the shop, but by 1968 M.E. Bodenham, the carpet specialist and furniture dealer, had moved in. During the 1970s Broadhurst Fabrics took the shop over and is still trading there today. Both the post box and the stamp vending machine are a reminder of the old post office. The stamp machine has been removed but the post box remains.

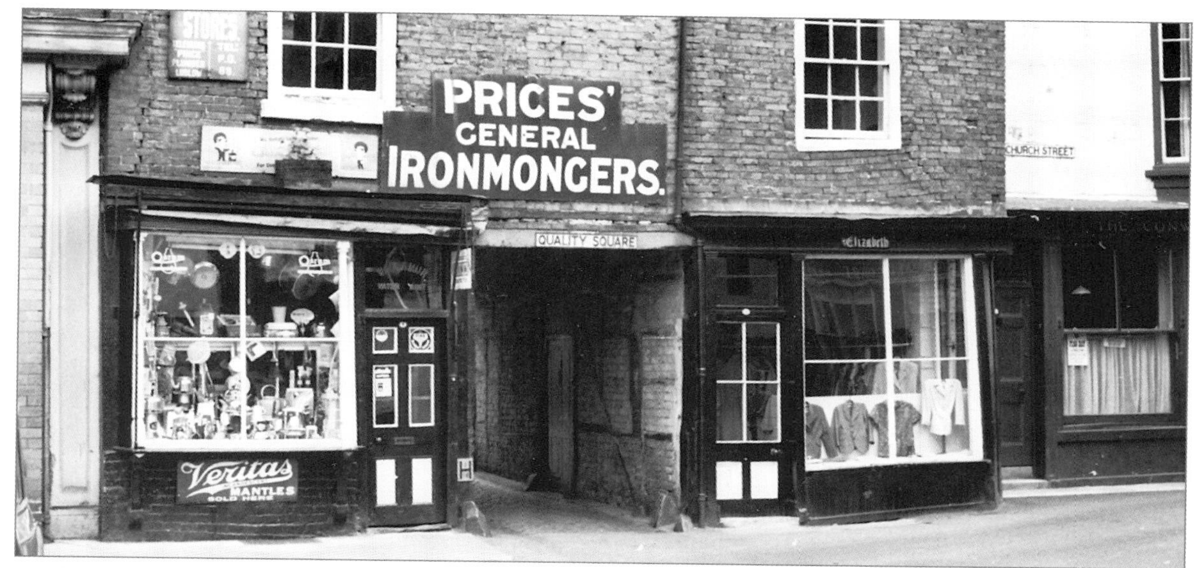

Quality Square takes its name from the houses of quality that were erected in the area. One of the finest was built mainly out of brick by Charles Fox, a wealthy lawyer who at one time served as secretary and clerk to the Council of the Marches. On the first floor is part of a long gallery that used to look out on to the courtyard, which is now the Square. This was William Price's first shop in Castle Street. In an advert for 1960 it was described as 'plumbers and water engineers, Calor Gas agents and expert fitters'. In the window is a fine array of household goods including kettles, frying pans, lamps and cooker sets. A teddy bear shop called Little Paws now occupies the building. The shop on the other side of the entrance sold women's wear and was called Elizabeth; today it is Antony Sheppard Ladies' Clothes.

The building to the right of Prices was erected in about 1900. For many years it was known as Castle House and was occupied by Meredith & Venables which was listed as a draper, silk mercer, dressmaker and milliner. In the 1930s the Ministry of Labour were at 24 Cove Street, before moving here. Today it is the Job Centre, and the ground floor has been modernised by being rebuilt in brick with a large central window and doors on either side.

CLOTHIERS BRADLEY'S OUTFITTERS
GYT
724

This is the south side of Castle Street looking towards High Street to the left of Bradleys and Market Street to the right. The building on the left is the Victorian town hall. At the bottom right is Woolworth's Store. On the ground floor of the tall four-storey building is the shop of W.S. Stephens who sold groceries and provisions. Moving to the right is the Castle Bookshop, then the bakery belonging to the Price family and on the right, in the ground floor of a Georgian town house, the Ludlow Speed Depot, whose motto was 'Betta Getta Vespa', which they could provide you with in 1960 for 125 guineas including purchase tax.

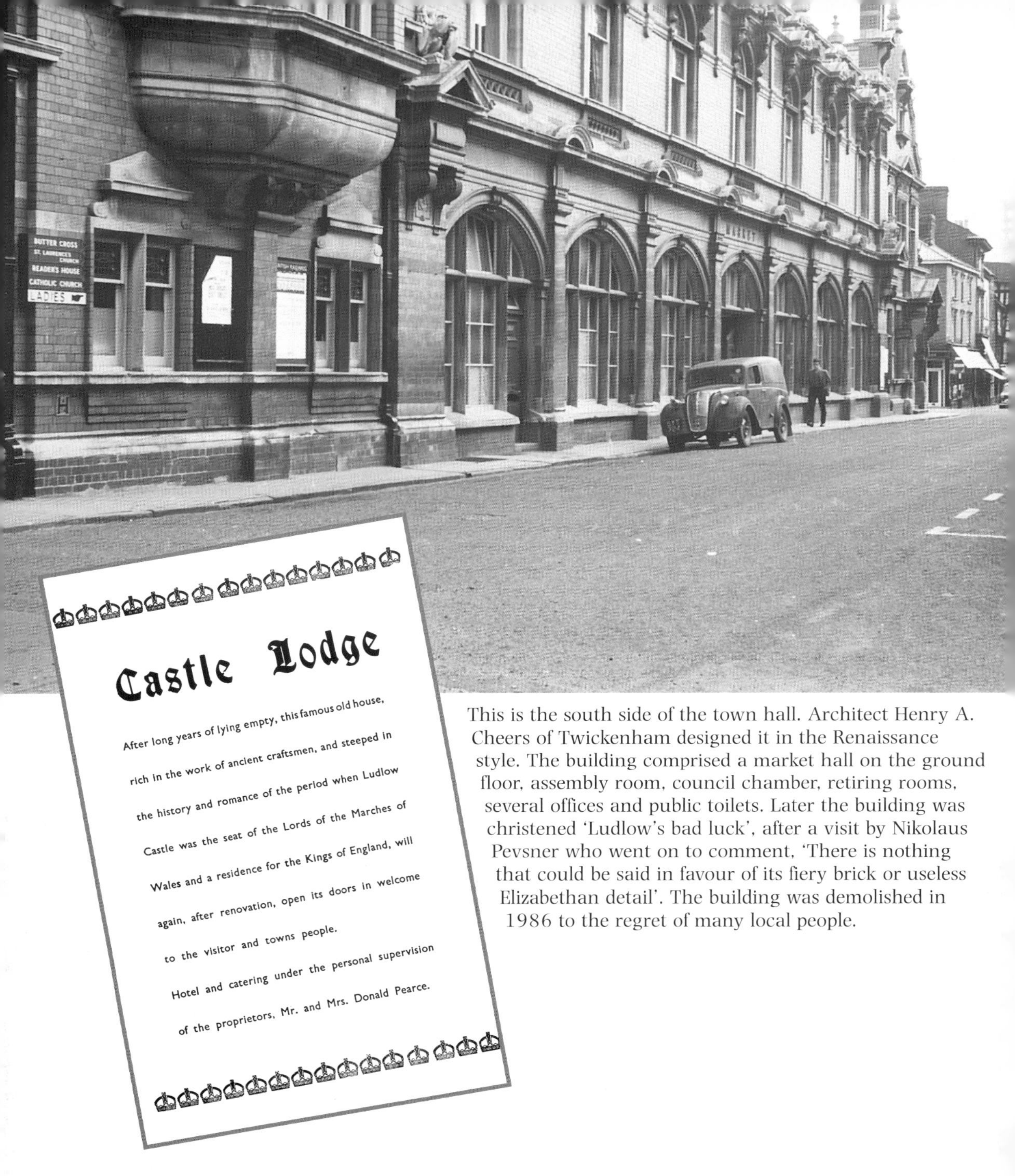

This is the south side of the town hall. Architect Henry A. Cheers of Twickenham designed it in the Renaissance style. The building comprised a market hall on the ground floor, assembly room, council chamber, retiring rooms, several offices and public toilets. Later the building was christened 'Ludlow's bad luck', after a visit by Nikolaus Pevsner who went on to comment, 'There is nothing that could be said in favour of its fiery brick or useless Elizabethan detail'. The building was demolished in 1986 to the regret of many local people.

Opposite, bottom: James Lang, a draper, once owned these premises standing on the corner of Castle Street and Raven Lane. He was there from about 1870 until 1930. In 1885 he was listed as a 'family draper, silk mercer and hosier'. The shop was also used at this time as a 'Cheque Bank Depot'. An educated man, Mr Lang was a Doctor of Science and Honorary Curator of Ludlow Museum. In 1930 the shop was transformed into a bazaar by F.W. Woolworth, selling all manner of goods at affordable prices. The store still trades from here today.

This is a view looking west towards Castle Gardens in the distance, with the town hall on the right and Castle Lodge to the left on the corner of Mill Street. With the removal of the town hall the site was left clear and now hosts a variety of open-air markets. The Lodge was used as a prison in the early part of the sixteenth century and was described as 'a hell' by criminals sentenced by the Council of the Marches. The lower section of the house was built in about 1564 for Thomas Sackford, an official of the Council. By 1960 it was known as the Castle Lodge Buttery and visitors were urged to patronise the business, which served 'A high class buffet service of good foods and a wide range of delicious drinks. The Buttery specially caters for visitors. It's a pleasure you cannot afford to miss. Personally supervised by Mr Donald Pearce.'

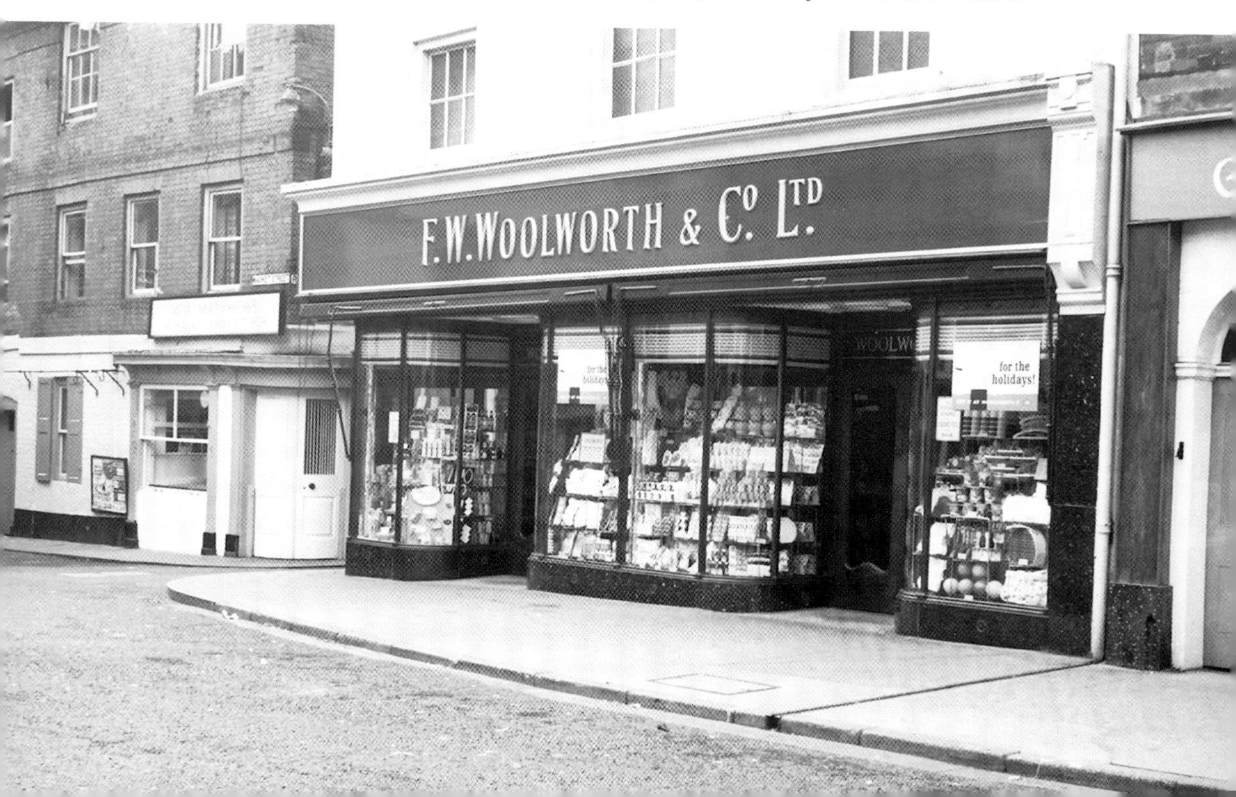

At the beginning of the twentieth century George Rix had grocery shops in Clun, Craven Arms, Bishop's Castle, Bridgnorth, Oswestry and Ludlow. As well as this shop in Castle Street he also had another in Old Street and by 1917 he had opened a butcher's shop in Broad Street. He also had a horse-drawn wagon to deliver groceries and provisions around the smaller villages and hamlets of south Shropshire, which could have been the county's first travelling shop. By 1960 W.S. Stephens had acquired the business and by 1968 he had other outlets in High Street and Tower Street. Today Cancer Research UK uses the premises.

Before becoming a bookshop this building was used by Francis Beeson, a dispensing, agricultural and photographic chemist. By 1960 Mr Bell was the owner of the Castle Bookshop. Today the shop flourishes and is well known for the comprehensive stock of books it keeps on local history and topography.

This shop has been a bakery for over a hundred years. At the end of the nineteenth century it belonged to Thomas Day, who was also a corn dealer. By 1905 Davies & Brown had acquired the business in Castle Street and also the Castle Mill. They continued to run the business until 1943 when Sidney Price bought it, and it is still run by his family today. In 1960 they were selling Procea bread for slimmers and a wide variety of confectionery. Note the board for Corvedale Motors Tours, and to the right of the window the sign for the Midland Red Parcel Agency.

This building was once used by solicitors Southern, Lloyd & Appleton who were Commissioners of Oaths, Clerks to the Governors of the Girls' High School and agents for the Alliance Fire & Life Assurance Co. In 1960 the premises had just become the Ludlow Speed Depot, moving there from the High Street. Bertie Green and his son were the proprietors and they invited the public to visit their new showrooms as they had something for everyone at competitive prices. Their stock contained mopeds, scooters, lightweights, 250s, big bikes, solos, combinations and three-wheeled cars. Note the Messerschmitt bubble car in the window.

Alfred Temple opened the Picture House in the Assembly Rooms in 1909. At first it was known as the Picture Hall and was an early example of a permanent cinema in a small county town. Alfred Temple bought the assembly rooms in 1920 and continued to run the cinema for many years. By the 1960s it belonged to the Craven Cinema Ltd, who that year advertised in this way: 'All your comforts catered for in South Shropshire's luxury cinemas, modernly equipped with the latest sound, projection and air-conditioning. You are cordially invited to visit the Regal Church Stretton, the Regal Craven Arms and the Picture House Ludlow.' Note the poster to the right of the main door; it is advertising *The Nun's Story*, starring Audrey Hepburn. It was being shown from Monday 1 August 1960 for twelve days on the cinema's new panoramic screen. Admission was 7*s* 6*d* for the front circle, 5*s* for the back circle, 3*s* 6*d* for the back stalls and 2*s* 6*d* for the front stalls. The café was available next door to supply film buffs with a quick snack before or after a performance.

The Most Central and Popular of all

CASTLE CAFE
AND SNACK BAR

Lunches
—
Teas
—
Suppers
—
Snacks
—
'Phone.
Ludlow 309

Open Daily 8 a.m. till 10.30 p.m.
(Sundays included)

SPECIAL TERMS FOR PARTIES

50 yards from the Castle and
adjoining the Car Park.

CASTLE CAFE

CASTLE STREET, LUDLOW.

The photographer is looking down Mill Street. The Assembly Rooms were opened on 2 July 1840 and were the centre for all the main social events in the area. The building was designed by Samuel Stead, a local architect, and was built on the site of the White Horse Inn. For a while the room on the corner was converted into a restaurant where members of the cinema audience could dine out after watching the film. Part of the ground floor is now the Tourist Information Office and, after spending some years in a building in Church Street, the Ludlow Museum is now housed there.

8

Mill Street

Mill Street runs parallel with Raven Lane and Broad Street. It leads down to the River Teme and the site of the town's first water mill, from which the street takes its name. On the right is Castle Lodge. After visiting Ludlow Thomas Churchyard later wrote in his book *Worthies of Wales* that this house was 'The faire house of Mister Sackford's, which he did build'. During the Civil War it was used to billet soldiers and later it was occupied by Robert Berry, who was a bailiff of the town on several occasions and also represented Ludlow in Parliament.

MORRIS
CASTLE GARAGE

The east side of Mill Street contains a number of fine eighteenth-century buildings. The white building at the top was a boys' day and boarding school run by Richard Thomas from about 1890 until the 1920s. Today it is called White Lodge and is the home of Arts & Antiques. To the right of the school was a public house called the Three Tuns, which was recorded from the second half of the eighteenth century. For a while it was known as the White Horse but had closed by 1870. In recent years it has been a private hotel.

Opposite: This building was erected at the same time as the Assembly Rooms to house the town's museum and the artefacts collected by the Ludlow Natural History Society, which was formed in the 1830s. At the beginning of the twentieth century for the price of 6*d* you could view a wide range of exhibits from British and foreign birds, fossils and minerals to relics from Ludlow Castle and prehistoric remains. By 1960 it was the showroom for Castle Garage, whose range of Morris cars comprised the Minor Saloon, Convertible and Traveller, the Cowley Saloon and the Oxford Saloon and Traveller. All models were powered by the new 'over-head valve engine for extra performance. They had big roomy interiors, stylish lines, attractive colours and safety glass all round.' Along with the Assembly Rooms this building has had a complete overhaul and the two are now linked, giving the community a complex worthy of the twenty-first century.

On the extreme left is the top section of the Guildhall, once the official office of the Palmers' Guild. It was renovated in 1768 when a new front was added. The buildings to the right are slightly earlier and were erected in 1713. The Guildhall is now used as a magistrates' court. The Blue Boar, which is reputed to be one of the first houses in the town to be built of brick, is still serving pints today. At first it was known as the Portcullis but in 1739 it changed its name to the Blue Boar, which it has remained ever since. The passageway to the left leads to the rear of the inn and also connects Mill Street with Dinham.

Opposite, below: Richards gift shop is housed in a Georgian building, which is dated on the downspout as 1740. A number of professional people moved their offices into some of the larger houses in the street and in the 1930s this building was occupied by William Tyrell, a solicitor, town clerk, clerk of the peace, advocate and commissioner of oaths. He was a partner in the firm Anderson, Son & Tyrell. K.W. Swift, who sells a fine selection of antiquarian books, maps and prints, now occupies the shop.

Just above the Blue Boar is the other part of the Castle Garage, whose showrooms were on the opposite side of the road. The business was founded in about 1930 when the proprietor was J.D. Parsonage. In 1960 they urged customers to 'Make it a Morris' as their range of cars were 'outstanding value in popular motoring'. The building had once been another public house known as the Hop Pole but was closed in the 1920s. Today it has been converted into offices for accountants Dyke, Ruscoe & Hayes and also serves as a branch of the Halifax.

ACKNOWLEDGEMENTS

I am very grateful to Simon and Giles Madin of Abbeycolor for allowing me to use the wonderful images they own of Ludlow in 1960. My thanks also to Robert Evans, Abbeycolor's black and white expert, who has once again provided me with excellent prints to use in this book. I would also like to express my gratitude to Bernard and Bill Cross who had the foresight to go out or send members of their staff to photograph the market towns of Shropshire in 1960. Last but not least I wish to acknowledge the staff of Shropshire Records and Research Centre, where all my inquiries are dealt with in a professional and friendly way.

BIBLIOGRAPHY

Baker, H., *An Alphabet of Ludlow Pubs*, H. Baker, 1985.
Baker, O., *Ludlow Town and Neighbourhood*, Simpkin, Marshall, 1889.
Cassey's Shropshire, 1871.
Hobbs, T., *The Pubs of Ludlow*, Logaston Press, 2002.
Kelly's Directories of Shropshire, various dates.
Lloyd, D., *Ludlow*, Chalford, 1995.
Lloyd, D., *Ludlow, The Second Selection*, Chalford, 2000.
Lloyd, D., *The Concise History of Ludlow*, Merlin Unwin, 1999.
Ludlow Advertiser, various dates.
Moran, M., *Vernacular Buildings of Shropshire*, Logaston Press, 2003.
Morriss, R. & Hoverd, K., *The Buildings of Ludlow*, Sutton, 1993.
Pevsner, N., *The Buildings of England – Shropshire*, Penguin, 1958.
Raven, M., *A Shropshire Gazetteer*, Michael Raven, 1989.
Shrewsbury Chronicle, various dates.
Weyman, H.T., *Ludlow in Bye-Gone Days*, Onny Press, 1972.
Wright, T., *History and Antiquities of Ludlow*, Morten, 1972.